D1505621

BEFORE THEY FADE

Preface by HRH The Prince of Wales

For over three centuries, the Royal Hospital at Chelsea has been home to thousands of men who have served their country in the British Army. Men who fought at battles such as Malplaquet, Corunna, Waterloo, Inkerman, Passchendale, the Somme, Tobruk, Burma, Anzio and Normandy. Each one has his own story to tell. This selection collected verbatim from men still living gives a deep insight into the life of a soldier, made even more vivid by their actual words.

BEFORE THEY FADE

BEFORE THEY FADE

by

The Chelsea Pensioners

Dales Large Print Books
Long Preston, North Yorkshire,
BD23 4ND, England.

British Library Cataloguing in Publication Data.

The Chelsea Pensioners
Before they fade.

A catalogue record of this book is
available from the British Library

ISBN   978-1-84262-645-0 pbk

First published in Great Britain in 2002 by
Royal Hospital Chelsea

Copyright © The Royal Hospital Chelsea

Cover illustration © The Royal Hospital Chelsea

The moral right of the authors have been asserted

Published in Large Print 2008 by arrangement with
Major Martin Snow, care of Royal Hospital Chelsea

All Rights reserved. No part of this publication may be
reproduced, stored in a retrieval system, or transmitted in any
form or by any means, electronic, mechanical, photocopying,
recording or otherwise without the prior permission of the
Copyright owner.

b11996365

LP 305. 906
BEF

WARRINGAH BL LIBRARY SERVICE

Dales Large Print is an imprint of Library Magna Books Ltd.

Printed and bound in Great Britain by
T.J. (International) Ltd., Cornwall, PL28 8RW

Acknowledgements

We would like to thank all those who have contributed their reminiscences to this collection. Not only for the gift of their memories and time in recounting them, but also for providing photographs and memorabilia for our use and finally for checking and correcting the finished work before printing.

In Memoriam

Jim Peart RVM   The Royal Horse Guards

To the Reader

The idea for the first collection of reminiscences originated from discussions between Martin Snow, a Captain of Invalids at the Royal Hospital Chelsea, and Robin Ollington, not only a friend of the Royal Hospital but one who has considerable experience in the world of design, writing and publishing.

As a result 26 reminiscences were collected, each with an interesting story to tell. Being a distinguished body of elderly gentlemen Pensioners are frequently interviewed by historians, journalists and television, particularly during the period of national remembrance.

We felt it might be of value to capture individual stories that the Pensioners themselves thought might be of interest and amusement to a wider public, and not necessarily confined to war or deeds of heroism. In other words, plain tales as told to the man in the street, and capturing something of the time at which they occurred.

The resulting book was well received, but with the passage of time sadly some of the original contributors have, unlike their stories, faded away. In true military tradition, however, others have stepped forward to fill the breach and we are now proud to present this second edition. As you will discover, as previously, some remarkable accounts have surfaced. It is worthwhile recording that none of these stories have ever been published before.

Martin Snow   Robin Ollington

CONTENTS

This small volume of reminiscences is respectfully dedicated to the memory of Her Majesty Queen Elizabeth the Queen Mother to whom the Chelsea Pensioners were 'My Gentlemen'.

In a world where it has become fashionable to rewrite history and belittle the actions and efforts of our predecessors, we sometimes need to recall what it was that they achieved.

I believe this modest book serves as a timely reminder of the service rendered to this country by a previous generation, and to highlight some of the exploits and experiences of that splendid body of gentlemen, the Chelsea Pensioners. They are truly the living embodiment of a bygone and less complicated age, when the simple virtues of honour, courage and selflessness were perhaps accorded a higher merit than they are today. The Gentlemen continue to represent the enduring qualities of service life – duty, discipline, and, above all, sacrifice. The nation owes them a debt which should never be forgotten.

I commend this book to you. You may well

be surprised by some of its contents and the breadth of human activity described, but most of all, I suspect, by its cheerful humility.

The proceeds of this book are being donated to the Royal Hospital Appeal and, as its Patron, I sincerely hope you will feel able to support this most worthy cause.

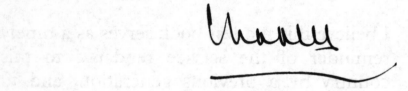

FOREWORD

by Antony Beevor

Napoleon's famous saying that 'an army marches on its stomach' may well have been true of the French. British regiments on the other hand seem to have fought and endured all the horrors thrown at them by falling back on their sense of humour. This excellent selection of reminiscences from the Desert War, Greece, Palestine, Normandy, the Low Countries, Germany, the Far East and Korea bring out the self-deprecating nature of the British soldier. Other armies who fought against us, and also indeed alongside us, sometimes thought that we did not take things quite seriously enough. This, of course, came from a serious misreading of the national character.

Many have argued that an army is the mirror image of the society it comes from, but that is only likely to be the case at times of mass conscription, such as during the First and Second World Wars. Today, of course, the ethos of the British Army with its essential beliefs in loyalty and duty could hardly be further from those of contemporary civilian life, where self-indulgence, the cult of the victim and egotism are now seen almost as inalienable rights. And yet over the last ten years we have seen an extraordinary revival of interest in the experiences of those who survived the terrible challenges of the Second World War. Journalists constantly ask why this paradox should have come about. There are a number of reasons and they are significant.

In 1995, after all the celebrations for the fiftieth anniversary of the end of the Second World War, most people – myself included – expected interest in the subject to collapse. But we were all wrong. During the course of the last decade we have been fast-forwarding into the future, accepting social and technological change as never before, yet the history of the Second World War has never been so popular in books, in films and on television.

No other period marked, changed or ended so many people's lives. The memory and experience was so intense for anybody who lived through it, that even today old men who may forget what they were doing a few hours before can vividly remember key wartime moments from over sixty years ago, as these passages show. But why should it also have such an effect on the young, three or four generations later?

I think it is because we now live in a post-military society, imbued with the mentality of a health and safety environment almost devoid of personal risk and moral decisions. Those brought up in this new civilian age are therefore fascinated by very personal questions influenced by what they read of war in today's newspapers: How would I have measured up? Would I have survived physically and mentally? And even: Would I have shot or mistreated civilians and prisoners?

Interestingly, a few years ago, a columnist in one newspaper complained at the surging interest in history and at the fact that so many novels now seemed to be set in the past. She felt that writers today should concentrate instead on contemporary issues. Another commentator at that time tackled the same subject but from a different direction. He observed that the reason for our interest in the recent past, especially the Second World War, came about because the key element in great fiction and drama was the element of moral choice. Today, he argued, we live in a non-judgemental society, with far fewer examples of moral choice, and so it was hardly surprising that writers should look to the past for their dramatic themes, as well as excitement and danger. The wartime generation lived at a time when individuals had hardly any control over their own fate.

Tastes and attitudes to history have followed wider changes. This has been particularly marked since the geo-political, financial, technological and social revolution of the late 1980s and 1990s, which broke down collective social structures and introduced a rampant individualism. History soon followed a similar route. In the past, historical subjects had always been treated in collective terms – the history of a country, an army, a division or a regiment. But a new generation which had shrugged off the ideals of collective loyalty suddenly wanted to know about the experiences and suffering of these individuals, caught up in huge events. This new generation, of course, is part of a post-Cold War society which knows virtually nothing of military discipline and conscript armies beyond what they see on television.

Ironically, interest in the subject of the Second World War has become so great that a belief has arisen in some academic circles that war is much too important to be left to military historians. The subject of warfare and armies is attracting outsiders to an unprecedented extent – sociologists, behaviourologists, anthropologists and cultural historians. I am all for diversity and there is nothing better than a good debate for shaking up ideas, but once a historical subject becomes a controversial bandwagon then one has to beware. History starts to suffer from the adversarial system. And this, as the Law shows all too well, is not always the best way of arriving at the truth.

Many newcomers to the broad field of military history are scrupulous in their background research and make a determined effort to overcome their lack of familiarity with the subject. Others, however, hope to apply a particular social or psychological theory while failing to understand armies or the true nature of war. This is the great danger of what one might term single-issue history.

It is for all of these reasons, and no doubt many more, that the memories of those who fought in the Second World War and Korea are so important. And the manner of their telling here should also be instructive in its essential modesty, straightforwardness and good humour. There can be no better corrective for those who see such institutions as the British Army and its regiments only in terms of caricature.

Bert Leach
The Worcestershire Regiment

Albert originally enlisted in the Royal Marines during the war in 1943 at Lympstone in Devon and remained with the Corps until demobilization in 1947.

However, he was not out of uniform for long, for in August of that year he put up the cap badge at the RASC at Yeovil which he joined as a driver, later being posted 'overseas' to the Isle of Wight for service with RASC Waterborne.

1948 saw a move to dry land in London as a member of the pool of Staff Car drivers based at Regents Park and it was there that he made what was to be an unforgettable and fascinating move to Fontainbleau outside Paris.

At that time the Chateau was the HQ of Commanders in Chief of the Western Union, later to become SHAPE under the command of none other than Field Marshal Montgomery.

With his background and experience,

when the C-in-C required a driver, the obvious choice was Albert and so for the next ten years until Montgomery's retirement it was Albert who drove the Field Marshal not only around his command in Europe, but also in the USA on official visits.

Obviously during this time he witnessed many important events as well as getting a personal insight into the character of this famous soldier.

In 1958, Sir Richard Gale not only took over from the Field Marshal, but also took over Albert who remained with him for three years, when once again he changed his cap badge on transferring to the Worcestershire Regt. with whom he served until 1968 leaving with the rank of Colour Sgt.

Civilian life saw employment in the retail trade and later responsibility for 5,000 properties for Havant Borough Council. But, the call of the uniform came once again and in 1998 he donned the familiar scarlet and blue at Chelsea Hospital where he related the following story...

The Field Marshal and the Footwear
Bert Leach

Unusually for a soldier's tale this begins in the luxurious setting of the Riviera in 1952 when I was driving Field Marshal Montgomery around the Allied units forming SHAPE and we were enjoying the comfort of the Hotel Metropole in Nice.

This gave me a wonderful opportunity to see the sights, promenades and shops of this famous town and one day I spotted a pair of very smart shoes with the then fashionable thick crepe soles. How proud I felt when I wore then with my civvies, and even prouder still when Monty himself admired them, indeed so much so that he asked me to get him a pair.

Duly purchased, he announced that they were so smart we should both wear them with our uniforms whilst on duty. Needless to say this decision did not go down well with his French ADC at the time, who obviously thought they were not quite the footwear for a Field Marshal.

Eventually we returned to Fontainbleau, where our style in footwear drew comment and was not regarded favourably, but being the Field Marshal nothing was said.

However, one day whilst visiting HQ at Versailles to collect petrol coupons, the sight of my non-regulatory footwear threw everybody into a fit. The RSM seized me and marched me in front of the CO who informed me I was improperly dressed and that I was to get back into regulation wear immediately. I didn't invoke the authority of the Field Marshal, indeed, would they have believed me? So dutifully changed back into army issue.

Returning to duty next day properly dressed, imagine my surprise when I was greeted by Montgomery almost in the manner of the RSM the previous day who demanded to know where my shoes were.

I related the tale of my visit to Versailles and the strict orders to revert to regulation footwear. Whereupon he immediately sent not only for the RSM but also the CO and in no uncertain terms informed them that 'nobody tells my staff what to wear.'

From then onwards the crepe shoes returned and on future visits to HQ the RSM ignored my presence and I and Monty enjoyed the comfort of 'our shoes' together for quite some time.

Tom Parnell
10th Royal Hussars

Born in Bolton, Lancashire, before the 'war to end all wars' ended in 1918, Tom's first employment was that of a cotton spinner in 1932. Three years later, like so many of his generation he enlisted in the T.A., in his case, the Duke of Lancaster's Own Yeomanry. 1936 saw a transfer to the Cavalry of the Line with an eventual posting to the Royal Dragoons at Hounslow, where after seven months training, including riding, he joined the regiment.

There then followed a posting to India and the North West Frontier to take part in what was then called 'showing the flag' exercises, riding out for several days.

With the eventual change from cavalry to armour, he underwent a conversion course to armoured cars and on the outbreak of war in 1939, the horses were left behind and he returned to England, and at Colchester in 1940 took over their iron replacements. Now a Troop Sergeant and ready to face the invader, he moved to Chippenham and there the regiment was issued with Valentine tanks.

Wishing to see more action, Tom volunteered for the Middle East. Action he certainly saw, for he was soon at sea again, this time bound for Suez via New York on board the Queen Mary, grey painted outside, but still luxurious within. Departure from New York was delayed whilst police investigated the theft of the ship's Royal Standard by American workers, and eventually they reached Africa. Here, instead of rejoining his old regiment, he found himself as a Troop Sergeant making up the strength of the 10th Hussars after Knightsbridge with its subsequent casualties, and now equipped with Crusaders and Honeys. Soon after, the battle of El Alamein was fought and it was during this that he, now in a Sherman tank, was wounded and blinded by a shell burst. Fortunately after nine weeks treatment his sight returned, as he did to the regiment, taking part in the advance upon Tripoli, Tunis and Algiers.

A proposed role in the invasion of Italy did not materialise, and instead with the 8th Army he landed at Tarranto in 1943 and fought up Italy to the Adriatic Coast at

Pissaro near the River Po where the war ended. At that point Yugoslavia boiled up with a dispute over Trieste and its ownership, so the regiment took over the role of a peace keeping force between the two factions.

November 1945 saw a move to Graz in Austria where as part of the appropriately named 'Operation Woodpecker' a more peaceful duty was performed, felling trees for the local population to provide timber for fuel and materials for rebuilding. Seven months later it was off again to Menden, Soest and Werl, this time with armoured cars (Daimler Staghounds), later replaced with American Chaffe tanks for border patrols at Lübeck in 1947.

Vehicles changed yet again to Comets in 1948, and an eventual return home to Tidworth with promotion to SQMS. With peacetime and the revival of the TA, he found himself with the Wiltshire Yeomanry as a PSI from 1954-56, after which he returned to Tidworth and eventual discharge as a SSM in 1958.

Having filled up everything from horses to armoured cars and tanks for twenty three years, Tom appropriately found work with Shell Mex BP as a Training Officer responsible for filling station staff, moving on to Elf Petroleum as both Training Officer and Internal Auditor until 1983.

Three years into retirement saw his arrival at Chelsea, where he has acquired not only responsibilities but also skill at wood carving. From time to time he has had the opportunity to re-cross the Atlantic, and not only visit the Queen Mary, but also to indulge his passion for horses by riding the trail and sleeping rough. Obviously then, the stories that follow are horse related.

Horse Sense and Horse Play
Tom Parnell

Horses have always played an important part in my life, both as a soldier, and now in retirement. Little did I realise as a young shaver of 27 in 1945 what an important role I would play in the future of some famous horses.

We had just moved to Graz in Austria from Trieste and were busy felling trees to supply fuel for the local population, when one day I was sent for by the Colonel and told that together with Sgt. Bill Deal, I should take two Bedford 3 Ton lorries and in the company of a local forester go with him and collect four horses. My immediate reaction was that we were perhaps going to collect polo ponies for the regiment which was famous for its polo playing.

However, two hours later and into the mountains, my supposition was proved dramatically wrong. We pulled off the road and went along a path to a cave. We were led into this by our guide, and there in a make-shift stable we saw to our amazement four of the world's famous Lippizaner horses from the Spanish Riding School in Vienna.

It appeared that at that time military zones were still in a state of flux with the Russians, an unknown quantity. General Patton, him-self a horse lover, feared that the Russians might appropriate these horses, or even worse, eat them or have the stable dispersed. We were, therefore, part of the plan to reunite and return them to Vienna. How do you get four such valuable horses into the back of a Bedford truck!

The solution was to back the trucks along-side the road and cut the bank away so that it became a slope up onto the truck. This we did after a lot of digging, and then covered the tailboard etc. with leaves to soften the approach. Two went in beautifully, but the other two took fright at the dark interior, and so we had to remove the canvas cover so they could see, and with tailboard up off we went to Vienna driving for two days along roads crowded with displaced persons and prisoners of war who must have been amazed at our load. We then spent several days at the Spanish Riding School living in the stables and eventually returned to duty – a job well done.

Fifty six years later this story has for me an even happier ending, for, during December 2001, the Spanish Riding School came to perform at Wembley, and through a mention in the press, the Austrian Ambassador got to learn of my story. As a result, one evening I was invited by him to attend a performance as his guest, and only on our arrival did I discover myself in the Royal Box announced as Guest of Honour, complete with spotlight, and the 'victim' of autograph hunters afterwards, and the recipient of a framed and signed photograph from the present riders of the school – a really memorable occasion.

A horsy story of a different nature occurred in 1953 after my return to Tidworth whilst working with the TA. As duty Sergeant Major, I had to be on duty with them at Tilshead by 6 a.m., and so it meant an early start by Land Rover across Salisbury Plain via Stonehenge. This July morning with the mists swirling around the stones, I did a double take as we passed by – was I seeing things, was it a ghost or was I hallucinating?

For there, perched high on the top of the stone arch, was a full sized wooden horse. We reversed to make sure we weren't mistaken, and it was then that I recognised the animal – it was our own practice polo pony! With that we raced back to camp and awoke the Adjutant and asked him if he knew where his pony was. At that time of the morning the answer is not really printable, but he said it was in the cage in which they practised. Inspection proved him wrong, and so before anybody, particularly the press and heritage authorities found out, we had to race out with out own lifting gear and retrieve it as soon as possible. Not quite the Trojan horse, but as we learned later, it was the Warwickshire Yeomanry who were at camp enjoying themselves at our expense having tipped off the Press in advance.

Finally, a story at my expense, or rather the taxpayers', which took place at Marlborough in 1955. At that time, I was a PSI at Devizes and responsible for moving the tanks over to the Plain for the T.A. to play with from time to time.

This particular day, instead of taking up position at the rear of the column in a Land Rover to record the damage that might be done en route so that compensation could be paid for damage to roads, kerbs etc., I decided to travel by tank.

As we swung round a corner into the wide and cobbled main street of this ancient town, our brakes failed, and 60 tons of Centurion tank started a slow motion slide, not only towards, but straight into the elegant Victorian facade of the local bank.

You can imagine the surprise of the manager as we crashed into his office with our .95 cannon ending up inches from his face, and our equal surprise at his response, said with hands up, 'Take the lot', a comment repeated at the Court of Enquiry but probably not received with the same amusement.

Ozzie Osborne MM
Commandos

Although he enlisted at 19 in the 70th Battalion (Young Soldiers) of the Welsh Regiment during 1941, it was by volunteering for the Commandos that he saw most of the action. Initial training took place on the Scottish coast at Largs and, wearing the familiar green beret with 3 Commando, his first experience of battle, or rather sight and sound of it, was the catastrophic Dieppe raid of August 1942. During this he had as a fellow shipmate on board the landing craft Jimmy Dix who is also an In Pensioner at Chelsea, and a contributor to this book.

Following Dieppe, like many others, he followed the trail to North Africa, trained for the attack on Sicily in 1943 and the landing at Agnoni, where a more than hot welcome was awaiting him in the shape of the 16th Panzer Division. Conditions there he remembered as far worse than at Dieppe and D Day.

Advances followed up the west coast of

Italy with various landings, finishing short of Naples, then a switch to the east coast, still living on board landing craft. Following the bridgehead at Termoli the unit was withdrawn to the U.K. in preparation for D Day.

This eventually dawned on June 6th with their arrival on Sword Beach complete with bicycles and with these the unit advanced quickly to Ambreville, eventually pushing on through the Low Countries to Germany, with Ozzie collecting en route a couple of wounds and the Military Medal.

Following the surrender of Germany, training began to tackle the Japanese, but the Atom Bomb put an end to that, and in July 1946, he rejoined the Welsh Regiment as part of Central Middle East Forces on the Italian Yugoslav border in what we would now call a peace keeping role. This lasted until December 1946 when he was finally discharged.

Civilian life for five years as a window fitter certainly lacked the excitement of past times, so it was into uniform again with the Malay Police as a Platoon Commander until 1961, when on returning home he went back to windows, followed by a spell in uniform once more as a traffic warden at Worthing, finally joining the Royal Hospital in 1999 where he recounted these experiences.

Green Berets and Bicycles
Ozzie Osborne

Having donned the former with pride, but still sporting the Welsh Regiment badge, I joined the ranks of the Commandos, and after training in Scotland found myself in August 1942 with 3 Commando bound with many others en route for the disaster called Dieppe.

Incidentally, some people wonder why Commandos never wear tin hats, only berets; this is not out of heroism or bravado, but because tin hats are heavy and get in the way, so it's out of practicality, not pride.

Anyway, embarking at Seaford into landing craft which were converted tank landing craft (LCT) armed with two 4 inch gun turrets, we set off across the Channel and were told that we would be ferried from the LCTs to the beach by small wooden barges.

All very well except that the enemy had spotted our Flotilla assembling sometime before, and so knew we were up to something. Accordingly, they were ready to greet us. As a result the E boats had played merry hell with the barges, many were sunk or damaged, and we in fact never left the ship. Instead we wallowed like a sitting duck off the coast being shelled and shot at, with casualties mounting and unable to do much in reply, except loose off from our own 'peashooters'. Churchill, I think, called it a fiasco, I could call it something else, but maybe the things learnt from this mistake helped with the eventual success of D Day. Incidentally, it was at Dieppe that the first American casualty in the North Western Theatre occurred, namely a U.S. Ranger Edwin Vincent Loustalot.

D Day was certainly a different kettle of fish – we had been reformed after Dieppe and its casualties, and Colonel Peter Young decided that each unit should have a parachute group. As I was a signaller at that time and not really combatant, I decided to have a go, and so volunteered for the paratroops. Having done all the training, fitness, jumping, etc. at the end, instead of being issued with parachutes, we were in fact given bicycles and told we had now become a bicycle troop.

Now, this may sound daft, but believe it or not they were great, for having got ashore at

Sword Beach on D Day, we were in fact in action seven miles away within a short time. We landed fairly easily, crossed the railway track and found the low lying land behind flooded for defence so ploughed through that and then stopped for a massive cycle clean before setting off along the road again.

Crossing the bridge at Benouville, we came under sniper fire and lost Guardsman Campbell. Brigadier Poett turned up and said our move towards Cabourg to pick up drops etc. was off, so we had better saddle up and move off towards Le Plein. This was up and over the ridge at Granville and along towards Ambreville along the coast road. Halfway along entering the built up area, Captain Roy Westley, O.C. 3 Troop, went off to recce and contact Colonel Otway. While he was gone who should turn up on a bicycle none other than Lord Lovat. I think he had taken poor old Campbell's bike. Anyway, he decided to send us up the road without benefit of recce and so we walked straight into an ambush.

A Russian medium machine gun opened fire and we could see a flat topped farm vehicle being used as a barricade. Firing my Bren from the hip, I shot the horses and carried on firing, changing magazines as I went. I suddenly realised that I was totally alone, the troop had buggered off leaving me engaging the enemy on my own. Grenadier Dixie Dean the No. 2 of the Bren had been shot, and feeling pretty angry I shouldered the gun and beat a hasty retreat down the road. Here it was suggested that we should go back and pick up the wounded, amongst them Dixie Dean who was dying and Johnny Abbot who had been wounded in the legs. As we bent down to pick him up, Sgt. Hill, who had accompanied me, was hit, as I thought, in the head. However, this was not the case for he appeared later having had his skull grazed by a bullet and falling unconscious.

Later on I carried out a recce with an officer, Keith Ponsford, and we managed to find a way into the town, attacked a row of houses and emerged with twenty prisoners – thus ended the battle of Ambreville, and my arrival on the shores of Mainland Europe.

Little did I think at the time that within a few weeks I would be standing before Monty in a quarry along the road to Cabourg to receive the Military Medal from him – so you could say I got a cyclist's medal with a difference.

Reg Fish
The Royal Warwickshire Regiment

A Welshman by birth in 1922, it was in 1936 that his family left Wales to seek work in Birmingham where Reg found employment as a metal polisher. Metal polishing of a different kind followed on his joining the 9th Battalion Royal Warwicks TA in May 1939 and four months later in September he was 'embodied' for active service. 1940/41 saw postings to Northern Ireland with promotion to Lance Corporal and Corporal, and then a spell in rural England at Berkhamstead and later at Frinton on Sea to repel invaders, plus live battle training at Cliftonville.

Promoted Sergeant in 1943, he volunteered for the West African Frontier Force and sailed from Liverpool in August 1944 via Gibraltar to Nigeria. Having native troops under his command obviously meant a command of their language, so back to school for a course in Hausa. There followed a posting to the Gold Coast as Platoon

45

Commander in 1944, travelling via Togo-land. After two months with the Training Battalion it was decided to send them to Burma, to join the 81st West African Division. Reinforcements of 3,000 African troops and 16 Europeans set sail for India and eventually saw action in Burma with the 5th Battalion of the Gold Coast Regiment. Withdrawn to India in 1945 to train for the assault on Akyab Island this was abandoned with the surrender of Japan, and he returned to Nigeria in February 1946 as CQMS not before, however, being involved in the mutiny of Gambian troops who expected to be demobilized and sent home as soon as the war ended.

In Nigeria his duties were to discharge and personally see over 504 troops returned to their villages. This completed, he returned to the UK and was literally discharged from the boat at Glasgow and returned to metal polishing, but not for long.

By December 1946 he was back in uniform with the Warwicks with sergeant's stripes up. After several courses it was back to West Africa again as a Platoon Commander with the 1st Battalion Gold Coast Regiment, where amongst other things, he had to deal with the Accra riots in 1948.

There then followed a spell back in England at Warwick where he became an Instructor in Musketry until 1951, when once again he was off overseas to Graz in Austria as a sergeant with the 1st Battalion Royal Warwicks – until they returned in 1953. He was promoted to WOII (CSM) in 1952.

He was then posted to the 5th Leicesters (TA) as a PSI followed by the 7th Warwicks (TA). This was followed by three years as a CSM at the Infantry Junior Leaders Regiment in Plymouth and a return to active service in both Aden and Hong Kong, returning home in 1960 for his last duties in converting a TA unit from a Light Anti-Aircraft role back to infantry. Thus, on January 29th 1962 he ended over 22 years service with the Royal Warwicks.

Civilian life saw him home in Birmingham, this time working for the Rootes Motor Group in various roles ranging from a car demonstrator to chauffeur to Lord Rootes, with a final move to Reynolds Tubes as Managing Director's chauffeur, and at retirement in 1974, Garage Manager.

Sixteen years later he again put on uniform, this time that of the Royal Hospital, but with particular pride in his cap badge.

A Fishy Tale or the Brigadier's Breakfast
Reg Fish

As we all know, fisherman's stories about the one that got away are legend. My particular tale, hardly a boast, is a little more deadly than usually heard, and rather than the traditional use of rod and fly, things were somewhat deadlier with the anglers themselves nearly ending up on the slab!

In 1947, whilst serving in West Africa with the 1st Battalion Gold Coast Regiment, we received a call one afternoon whilst out in the field to say that the C.O. had the Brigadier coming to breakfast the following day, and would like to offer fish on the menu – could we oblige?

So a fishing party was assembled, myself, European CSM Rocky Knight from the D.L.I. and a Lt. Michel from French Togoland, one of the first black officers to be commissioned.

No rods, keep nets or gaffs for us, simply a box of grenades and a jeep. In this we set off to the banks of the River Niger in search of our quarry. Arriving as darkness fell, we drove up to the river bank, switched on our headlights and launched our inflatable boat.

Reaching what we thought was deep water, Lt. Michel suggested we each throw a grenade over the side. His plopped nicely down into the depths. However, deceived by the light of the headlights on the water, we assumed it was all deep, but my grenade only sank a short distance on to a sand bank in the middle of the river. The result was somewhat dramatic and painful; huge spouts of water, shrapnel and sand.

Lt. Michel shouted out that he had been hit in the back, the boat started to deflate and sink. Knowing that the river was infested with crocodiles, I grabbed the paddle and struck out for the bank, only able to use my right arm as the other was numb and failed to respond.

Fear and determination got us to the bank, and Rocky hauled us out and drove us a very painful twenty five miles back to camp. Here conditions without electricity weren't ideal for medical treatment, and after initial repairs by the light of smelly hurricane lamps, the M.O. decided to send me to hospital at Kumasi. No blue lights and sirens, but a two day journey over 237 miles. I had sustained shrapnel damage to my back, knee and left arm which had left the hand paralysed. Some of it was extracted, but because of the conditions prevailing, it was not all removed, and I carry it as a souvenir today, but with time and care my hand regained its use.

Needless to say the Brigadier went without his breakfast, and the explanation for the escapade given to the ensuing Court of Enquiry perhaps could be regarded as rather fishy. Lt. Michel recovered, and later went on to make his name as the first black Equerry to H.M. The Queen.

Another brush I had with names that were later to make history, was in 1948 at Accra, when we were sent to deal with the riots. I had the job of putting the two ring leaders under close arrest. Little did I realise at the time that my two prisoners were later to play an important role in the future of Ghana. Dr. Dankwa and Kwami Nkruma, the latter becoming the first President of Ghana.

Another historical event, this time in the military sense, was also in 1948, when in November the news of Prince Charles' birthday came through. Being an infantry unit, we had no artillery to fire a Royal Salute, therefore it fell to me to arrange a 'feu de joie'. This is an incredibly complicated, but amazing movement in which the salute is fired in a ripple effect by two ranks of riflemen – a sort of explosive 'Mexican Wave' I would imagine, but probably not executed for many years before, and I would think, has never been performed since, but for me, a memorable experience which I have always associated with November 14th every year since.

Jim Peart RVM
The Royal Horse Guards

From the age of 16 Jim followed in his father's footsteps as a miner, but upon reaching 18 in 1930 and standing at six feet, he decided that life underground at Easington Colliery was not for him, and so he joined the Colours.

With his height and hearing, these turned out to be those of the Household Cavalry, and after training he was posted to the Royal Horse Guards taking part in all the duties associated with that historic regiment, ranging from Trooping the Colour, King's Guard and Sovereign's Escort at the 1937 Coronation of King George VI.

The outbreak of war in 1939 saw the end of plumes and breastplates, and with 800 horses, they set off on a journey across France to Marseilles and an eventual destination of the Syrian frontier via Palestine.

A return to Egypt embarked on the famous duo of destroyers, Achilles and Ajax of River Plate fame, led to a journey through the

Med to Piraeus sinking a U Boat en route.

Mount Olympus saw a different sort of activity than athletics, for in 1941, with the Aussies, the regiment held the front line, with an eventual withdrawal via Thebes across the Corinth Canal through Athens, ending up at Kalamata where an Austrian bullet put an end to any further activity and a new role 'annoyingly' as a prisoner of war.

This Jim didn't take kindly to, and on arrival at Stalag VIIIB, he made several attempts to escape with the inevitable punishment, and finally in 1944 he was despatched to the notorious camp at Ausvitz in Poland and work in coal mines.

By 1945 with the Russians putting pressure on the Germans, it was decided to move all prisoners away from the front. Thus began a gruelling march of over 800 miles, crossing the Carpathian mountains twice and seeing the horrors of Dresden en route.

Liberation came in the form of the American 3rd Army and repatriation to the UK by air from Rheims. The 6'2" soldier at 14 stone now weighed only 8 stone, but after patching up and feeding, returned to service with breastplate and plumes dusted off.

Duties now included the Queen's wedding in 1947 and riding at her Coronation in 1953, 17 years after he had done so for her father, and thus it continued until 1961 when retirement seemed the order of the day.

Little did he think that 25 years later, he would still be serving the Sovereign as a member of the Queen's Bodyguard with the rank of Yeoman Bed Manager, awarded the Royal Victorian Medal amongst 8 others – a far cry from the dirt and dust of the pit all those years ago.

Still a member of the Queen's Bodyguard, but on the non-active roll, he has been at Chelsea for 2 years, and elaborates on his life in the following pages – a story which would perhaps make even Steven Spielberg gasp with incredulity!

These reminiscences appeared in the original edition and are now published posthumously in memory of Jim Peart who died whilst this second volume was being prepared.

Pomp and Different Circumstances
Jim Peart

Although a serving soldier for many years, the following stories in fact come from a period when as a prisoner of war, I was unable to carry out my role as I had hoped.

So we begin in 1941, when at Kalamata in the Southern Peloponese a rather unfriendly Austrian put an end to my active participation in the war by shooting me through the chin, shoulder and left leg, and in this condition I ended up in the 'bag'.

Being wounded, I was taken to a makeshift hospital in Piraeus tended by the Sisters of Mercy. Here it was decided that as my leg showed signs of gangrene, it should he amputated and the doctors actually drew the cut line around it ready for the surgeon.

However, this was not to be, for an Aussie RAMC Unit put into port knowing full well that they would become prisoners, but the call of duty and the many wounded was far more important to them, and thanks to them my leg was saved.

Plastered up, and with the introduction of maggots to feed on the wound, a cure was eventually effected which enable me to cope with what was to follow.

At this point I witnessed perhaps my first sight of the inhumanity of war, which I have never forgotten. As we marched towards the railhead for transportation to the prison camp, a young Greek girl came out and offered us grapes, whereupon the guards seized her by the hair, trussed her up, and, together with her mother, dragged them along with us. Overnight they were strung up, and as dawn broke we were horrified to discover that they had both died in the night.

Our journey to Stalag VIIIB by train, or I should say cattle truck, was horrendous, packed in so tightly that nobody could sit. The relief came when some poor unfortunate died and dropped to the floor, and we eventually ended up sitting on piles of our fellow travellers. During this journey we were never let out, had only one small loaf to eat, no water, and other conditions which I will leave to your imagination.

Eventually arriving at Stalag VIIIB at Lambsdorf in Upper Silesia we were stripped of our clothes, labelled and put into open fields for the night where we slept sitting back to back; in some cases, never waking up. Then followed the statutory head shaving, mixed delousing in company with some

Ukranian women, token clothing, and then banged up behind the wire.

Food was appalling, black bread and so-called soup. On one occasion I remember the cooks calling out if anybody wanted some more. A massive stampede followed, and one poor soul fell into the vat of soup and was scalded to death.

During the day we were sent out into the surrounding forests to work, so dense that it was like night. Here we planted and felled trees, cleared scrub, etc. At this point I decided it was time to make a move, and made several attempts at escaping to join the resistance.

My longest spell of freedom was six weeks, terminated through my own stupidity, when having taken all my clothes off to dry them, I decided to have a brew up and lit a fire. Needless to say, an eagle eyed forester saw the smoke, and I was recaptured, as one would say 'in the buff'. Punishment duly followed, and I spent 9 months in solitary confinement. This is not nearly as bad as that meted out to a young Welshman who tried to escape by dashing through the closing gates. He was shot and discovered next day dressed in civilian clothes in a cesspit. The story told to a neutral investigator being that he was caught escaping in these clothes and shot – no little bending of the truth.

Punishment of a different sort was decided for one of our civilian foresters who had taken a distinct dislike, not only to one, but other members of our group. His cruelty knew no bounds, and reached the heights of evil, when one day, one of the party, Cpl Horibin of the 4th Hussars, who had trouble with his back, had difficulty getting up from the hole in which he had been working. This forester spoke to the guard who unbelievably, without any compunction, simply bayoneted him. To say the least we were horrified by such an open atrocity and vowed revenge. The opportunity came a few days later when we were sent to fell a 35 metre fir tree that was leaning towards the phone wires.

Our 'favourite forester' led the party giving strict instructions as to which direction the tree should fall. The 'axemen' in every sense were a mixed bunch of Aussies, New Zealanders and Maoris to whom the forester had taken a particular dislike.

With razor-like axes they felled not only the tree, but with it the forester who vanished beneath its weight, never to give orders again!

Retribution was swift; a court-martial, thrown into the cells at the SS barracks in Breslau for 6 weeks to sleep on stone floors with only a blanket and little food.

There were perhaps lighter moments, and I approach this story with some hesitation, but it did happen, and seemingly without any ill-effects. The German Officers' Mess at the camp was being rebuilt, so their kitchens were 'kaput' and meals were prepared in the prisoners' cookhouse. Soup was on the menu, and we were detailed to carry large billycans on poles across to the Mess. Needless to say their food was much better than ours, and so, en route we stopped and helped ourselves to a mug or two. However, with the thoroughness of Germans, they soon spotted that the amount was decreasing and the Kommandant sent for me said any more of this pilfering and we would be for it. So on our next trip, we once again stopped for refreshment, but this time made up the missing quantity from a source that I leave you to guess! Next day I was sent for by the Kommandant and feared that we had been rumbled – instead he told me that he was glad that we had stopped pilfering, but it was in his words 'prima' soup!

The Forests and life in a Stalag were, however, exchanged in November 1944, for Poland and a notorious camp in Silesia where once again I found myself underground as a miner, black, filthy and with the flimsiest of clothing and little food. News eventually came through of the Russian advance, and with it the decision for all prisoners to be moved away from the front line.

So in January 1945, thousands of us, men, women and children, political prisoners, Jews, Ukranians, Russians, you name it, began a slow and dreadful march across country. Needless to say the journey took its toll as people died, were shot, and even strafed in the forests by the Allies, thinking we were a German column. Again humour of a sort enters the story. I once sat by a hen for four hours waiting for it to lay an egg, which I ate, followed by the hen which I shared with my pals. At one time we bought a donkey, nicknamed Benny, for a bar of chocolate. It served us well, though somewhat reluctantly at times, to carry our sparse belongings, and eventually made the supreme sacrifice by dying and feeding quite a few of us for a day or so.

The weather was appalling and so cold

that sleeping in the open only became possible when three of lay side by side; the middle one being warmed by the two on the outside so that he could sleep. So every third day we got a little sleep, though this was interrupted by the hunger of the lice who surfaced with the warmth to feed on our already emaciated bodies.

During this march we in fact crossed the Carpathian mountains twice, witnessed the result of the Dresden bombing, and in total clocked up over 800 miles on foot.

Enough was enough, and four of us decided to part company with this dreadful crocodile. When an opportunity presented itself, we hid up, let them pass, and under cover of darkness crept off, moving across country at night. Food and shelter were paramount, and eventually we came across an isolated farm which we broke into, tying up the farmer and his wife and daughter whilst we found a gun, ammo and binoculars. Then, untying the wife we got her to get out her frying pan, and it may seem extraordinary, but we polished off seventy eggs and bread between us. We then set ourselves up in a barn, and amongst other things, acquired a Mercedes and petrol, and as the populace had fled, began to recover ourselves, but keeping a low profile.

All went well until one day we heard the rumble of tanks, and looking out saw an American column approaching. Knowing that the bridge was mined, I rushed out to warn them. Imagine my surprise when I found myself with hands up calling out to none other than General Patton not to shoot me and not to cross the bridge.

The Americans dealt with it and rolled on, and we were taken to Landschutz and flown to Rheims, en route passing over the devastated city of Cologne. At Rheims we were to fly with the RAF back to the UK. Here we found thousands of lads queuing for a place in the Halifaxes that were to take them to 'Blighty'. At last I got to the door of a plane only to be told it was too full. Here fate stepped in once again, and reluctantly I retook my place in the queue, only to hear later that this particular aircraft had crashed on landing at Croydon and all on board had been killed.

So ended my war – not what I had expected at the start, but one that has given me a great insight into human nature, both good and evil, and a memory which has enabled me to retain and relate some of these experiences for you.

Charlie Hackney
Special Air Service

A 'Brummie' by birth in 1917, Charlie enlisted in the Royal Signals (TA) in April 1934, and a year later joined the 15/19th Kings Royal Hussars. With them he did his basic training at Shorncliffe before being sent to an outpost of the Empire on the North West Frontier with the 13/18th Hussars.

During his spell in India he transferred to the 16/15th Lancers and returned with them in 1940 to join the BEF in France and deployed to Arras. Heavy fighting with casualties took place, amongst them Charlie who embarked from the crowded beaches of Dunkirk on board a destroyer for hospitalisation at Dover and an eventual move to Colchester.

On recovery he joined 48 Tank Battalion and volunteered for service with the Commandos and joined 5th Commando at Bridlington for training. This was put to the test in a dramatic raid on German installations on the Lofoten Islands in Norway.

As a member of the Royal Armoured Corps he was then ordered to Bovingdon and underwent a six week driving, gunnery and wireless course on Crusader tanks. Having mastered this it was off to North Africa and the 8th Army in the desert. At Alexandria they collected the tanks they had brought with them, and were ordered to the 4th Hussars. He was promoted to tank commander from corporal. On arriving at HQ 4th Hussars, he and two other tanks were sent up the line to reach the 4th Hussars who were sadly depleted due to enemy action.

The tanks, however, could not stand up to the enemy fire power, and as a result his two vehicles were destroyed. The SAS was recruiting at this time and with a thirst for adventure, he joined their ranks and saw action with the LRDG and the SAS with 'Paddy' Mayne and eventually with Bill Stirling and Major Roy Farran in 2nd SAS.

Malaria and Sand Fly fever put him out of action for a while, but he was soon hack in action travelling by submarine to Pantalaria to blow up the lighthouse followed by the Tarranto landing and the advance to Termoli where on meeting up with the 1st SAS he returned to the UK with them as his mother had died and he had family responsibilities. Those sorted out he returned to duty and rejoined 2 SAS, and went like so many to Scotland to train for the Second Front.

However, it was behind German lines parachuted into France to join the Resistance that he found himself, details of which follow in his story. Back from France he again began training, this time for a waterborne Rhine crossing which was carried out successfully with a follow-through to Luneburg, scene of the eventual German surrender.

About to withdraw at the end of hostilities to the UK and eventual deployment to Norway, the unit was suddenly flown there overnight. However, on route the Germans surrendered, so on arrival at Stavanger they moved on to Bergen to mop up any German resistance and also the Quislings who had aided the enemy.

This achieved, it was back to England, followed by demob in 1946 and civilian employment with Rolls Royce and the Yarrow Admiralty Research Department.

In May 2000 he joined the ranks of the other long serving soldiers at Chelsea.

'Hitting the Enemy Just Where it Hurts Most ... Up the Arse' *General Le Clerc*
Charlie Hackney

I was operating with No 1 Troop, No 1 Squadron in France in 1944 with Lieutenant Mike Pinci. My job was to escort him to Maquis conferences as his bodyguard. On this occasion we went to a barn near Epinal where several top Maquis people were expected. The conference had begun by the time we arrived and the barn was quite full. There was a sudden commotion and a member of the Maquis produced a pistol, shouted Lieutenant Pinci's name and fired at him. I shouted to Mike and lunged at him, knocking him flying. All hell broke loose and about half a dozen Maquis men grabbed the gunman and hustled him out of the barn. Shortly after I heard a couple of pistol shots. I learned afterwards that he was a member of the Milice and had been collaborating with the Germans.

On another occasion I was escorting Lieutenant Mike to visit some friends and an uncle of his north of Epinal. Mike had commandeered an old German staff car and after about 15 miles we came to a sharp 'S' bend in the road. We were doing about 60 miles an hour and Mike operated the brake pedal to slow us down. No response! Frantically Mike tried to steer the car round the bend but we went into a spin and turned over. I was thrown out with the Bren gun and was lucky to escape with nothing worse than a badly bruised back. Mike was knocked out but came to after a few minutes and we decided to leave the car where it was and complete our journey on foot. His uncle greeted us with open arms and we had a terrific feast. After the meal we returned to the accident spot where Mike's uncle had rounded up some mechanics to look at the car. They discovered that someone had tampered with the brakes. We never discovered who but we were forbidden to travel in it again and were sent back to hide in the forest of Chatillon.

I also took part in one of Mike Pincis more successful operations where we destroyed 40,000 gallons of high octane fuel destined for German fighter planes stationed in Chatillon. The local intelligence we had been given by the Maquis was incomplete, but we set out on a beautiful Sunday morning and set up a good ambush position on a winding piece of road and settled down to wait for the convoy. I can remember that a few people were on their way to Mass in Chatillon and I can still see the little girl who stopped to pick some flowers from the side of the road. We were all very keyed up and were praying that these people would disappear before the convoy came into sight. At last they went – just in time as a scout signalled that the convoy was approaching. I was to spring the ambush by firing the first shots from the Bren. Trooper Stackhouse was my loader and as we opened fire I can recall vividly bits of cloth flying off the German driver and his mate as they were hit. The convoy consisted of five fully loaded tankers with four motor cycle escorts and three trucks loaded with German troops. We killed them all. We pulled out 'toute suite' afterwards and as we had run out of ammo the jeep was much lighter than before. I can remember afterwards seeing a column of thick black smoke from 15 miles away.

I was sent out with a foot patrol a few days later and when I came back I heard that Mike had been killed on the way to Paris to see his father who was the San Marino Ambassador to Paris. Ironically he had commandeered another German staff car and had been shot up by a British fighter plane on the lookout for just this sort of target. We recovered his body and it lay in state in a church in Chatillon where we all went to pay our respects to a very gallant officer and gentleman.

Serving with Mike Pinci for me was one of the most exciting and rewarding times of my life. I am particularly proud of the fact that this relationship and my work with him was recognised at the end of the war when I had the honour of receiving the Croix de Guerre in Paris from none other than General Le Clerc, Commander of the Second French Armoured Division whom I had earlier encountered following a successful attack on the Germans at Langres railway station.

Bill Moylon
The Royal Iniskilling Fusiliers

Bill is from Newport, Gwent, where he was born during the Great War in 1915. Twenty four years later working as a fitter for London Transport, he himself went to war, volunteering for the Royal Army Service Corps. However, as their ranks were full, he found himself in 1940 en route to Belfast to join the 407 Holding Battalion of the Royal Irish Fusiliers. Training completed, and with the post Dunkirk shortage of men, he was posted to the 6th Battalion of the Royal Iniskilling Fusiliers. This Irish connection lasted until May 1941, when with his engineering background he was transferred to the Royal Army Ordnance Corps.

With them, the stories related on the following pages began, invoking as they do memories and places both exotic, divers and horrific, including Canada, South America, Trinidad, South Africa, India, Burma and finally Thailand and Cambodia.

When peace finally came in 1945 with his

return to the UK and recovery from his experiences, Bill married the girl who had been waiting for him and settled into civilian life.

Returning to London Transport, he found himself somewhat unusually, due to the shortage of accommodation, living on Kingsway Tube Station. However, this did not last long, and he returned to his native Wales to work for the aluminium giant Alcan for the next 35 years (14 as a long distance lorry driver and the remainder as a supervisor). Little did he think as he used to drive along the Chelsea Embankment on his trips to London, that one day he would end up as a Chelsea Pensioner. This he did in March 1998 after the earlier death of his wife, and his own decision not to be a burden to his son.

Now as a Hospital NCO Bill Moylon leads a very full and active life, and able to indulge two of his passions, travel, and still keeping in step as a ballroom dancer.

A Guest of the Emperor
Bill Moylon

In 1941, I found myself on a convoy out of

Liverpool bound for Halifax, Nova Scotia, and from thence on an American troopship which sailed to Capetown via Trinidad. We were made most welcome in South Africa – indeed so much so that the Fifth Column tried to encourage British soldiers to desert. During this time the Japanese had attacked Pearl Harbour. We sailed for Bombay as 18 Divisional Workshop RAOC, having been originally destined for the Middle Eastern theatre (our vehicles, perhaps predictably for the situation then prevailing ending up in Mombasa!) From thence we sailed for the Far East, exact destination unknown, on the Empress of Asia, an old three-funnelled coal burner, escorted by HMS Exeter (of River Plate fame) and two destroyers. Conditions for the 3000 troops on board were atrocious, the food appalling and the crew had raided the canteen. We were bombed by the Japanese and straddled, but emerged unscathed. A second bombing attack brought the unreliable crew up on deck and the ship stopped for lack of engine power because the stokers had mutinied. This time we were a sitting duck, and before long the Japanese had machine-gunned the lifeboats on their davits and the ship had sustained five or six direct hits on the superstructure. Soon the ship was ablaze and covered in a dense black smoke. The order to abandon ship was given and I, and my good mate Pat Regan donned our life jackets and jumped over the side. I never saw him again. I made it to a life raft, and after 3 or 4 hours in the water, we collected about 50 people before being rescued by an Indian gunboat, the 'Sutlej'. We were landed at Singapore and kitted out with the most basic equipment and weapons before being sent into action as infantry. Not long afterwards Singapore surrendered.

We were marched 16 miles to a POW concentration area at Changi where very quickly we went on to a rice-only diet and started to experience severe dietary problems. Rice is 70% water and practically no bulk, and that and the insanitary conditions soon brought many fit and healthy men low. There was also no salt to be had. In truth, at that time the Japanese simply had no notion of how to cope with so many prisoners and we were left rather to our own devices, working on the docks and so on working for the Japs.

I was in the first party to leave Singapore in May 1942 in railway trucks for Ban Pong in Thailand, 36 to a truck and not room for all to sit simultaneously. Later at Nong Pladuk we had our first experience of gratuitous Japanese brutality, men being beaten for no reason at all. We decided to go on strike, an action unheard of at the time and probably never repeated. The Japanese reaction was to bring in troops who covered the POWs with machine guns and forced us to stand in the broiling sun for 12 hours where we were literally cooked alive. Eventually I joined a working party of 140 to set up transit camps for prisoners who were sent to work on the Burma railway. We were told before we went that there were no prison fences – the jungle was the barrier and there was no way out. On the 4 day trip by sampan we were capsized on the river Kwai and lost even our meagre possessions. Of the 140 who set out, 40 died.

We were separated from the main camp of 7000 POWs engaged in supply details which gave opportunities for pilfering badly needed items. I remember a hospital building in the main compound outside which was a small structure with no side walls into which prisoners were carried from the main building to die. We caught lizards to supplement our meagre rations. I recall a native camp approximately one mile from our camp, where dead bodies were simply heaped into an open pit and covered with a thin layer of earth which sank as the bodies decomposed, leaving room for further layers.

We were sent to construct a wooden bridge over the Kwai river. The Japanese were first class bridge builders but conditions were deteriorating all the time. The Japanese simply wanted to get the railway built in order to get their supplies up country for the attack on India. Human life ceased to have any real value. There were no mechanical tools – 400 kilometres of railway were built by hand and POWs were regarded as expendable. The Japanese were simply not able to look after them properly, even if they had wanted to do so. There were no supplies, no medical facilities, no clothing – just a loin cloth and wooden sandals called 'clompers' we made ourselves after our army boots had disintegrated. We worked 12, 15 or maybe 18 hours a day. The Burma Railway was started in June 1942 and finished 15 months later. It was never used properly because the Allies kept cutting it and my one abiding thought is of so many fit young men dying for such a useless effort.

I was on the railway until October 1943 when I was moved to a camp at Tamakan where I recall having to dig a perimeter trench 20 feet wide and the same depth. This I knew was to be a mass grave as the Allies were getting the upper hand. The death rate was in any case enormous.

I was picked as part of a working party to build an airfield, in direct contravention of the Geneva Convention and this entailed working in a quarry. All the drilling for blast holes was done by hand, the sick holding the drill steady while the 'fit' hammered it into the rock. After the charges were set off, each team had to break 1.5 cubic metres of rock for the runway, and the Japanese measured the amounts. Woe betide anyone who had not fulfilled their quota! In early 1945 I was moved to another camp near the border with Cambodia containing 4-5000 POWs. Again, in flagrant contravention of the Geneva Convention we were put to work building perimeter fences and gun emplacements. There were two old lorries which could not function for lack of petrol so the engines were removed and they were used, with human pulling power, to take supplies to a large Japanese troop concentration some 8 miles away in the hills. Having dug further trenches and gun emplacements we then returned to our own camp dragging the lorries, now full of fire wood.

It was now evident that the end of the war was in sight and rumours abounded. We heard that a bomb had been dropped in Japan but no one knew the significance of this then. The Japanese guards suddenly become very passive. Ordinarily we were roused every morning to the Japanese bugle call for 'Reveille' and one morning we woke to the British call. We then realised that our long nightmare was at last over. The Japanese had vanished overnight, and after a day or so doctors were parachuted in together with medical supplies, food and clothing. After a week or so Lady Mountbatten visited us and our officers joined us. I was taken to Bangkok where I met General Bill Slim, to Rangoon where I was introduced to Lord Mountbatten and spent some time in hospital there before beginning the journey home. I went via Ceylon and Suez and was beginning to put on weight before eventually arriving at Southampton, and then to Newport, and so ended my war. Obviously such memories never fade and return again and again. I have in fact returned to Japan as part of the 'reconciliation' initiative. And although I do not consider myself an emotional man, or one given to deep introspection, I will carry with me always the memory of tragic and unnecessary waste of young lives. It wasn't even a sacrifice because that implies an achievement, something you can be proud of; it was just a waste, a sheer bloody waste.

Bill Moylan has asked that this account be dedicated to the memory of all those comrades who died on the Burma Railway as well as to those who, as a result of their treatment, have suffered and died since then.

The poem that follows was copied by Bill in 1944 on a scrap of paper intended as a cigarette wrapper. 'Good job they never found it' he muses. 'They executed men for less'.

There's a camp of ghostly horrors to the north of
  Kanyu II
There are scores of bamboo crosses in the mud
And they mark the place where hundreds lie –
  where once the jungle grew
In rest that was denied them while they lived.

It was known what men could do by the docs at
  Kanyu II
That the place was hot and it was bound to tell
So they warned the yellow cranks of the
  thinning of the ranks

78

And the colonels made a fuss of it as well,

Men had striven hard and long with a courage
  that was strong
That they had died thro' over work was plain to
  all
Some were barely twenty-one, yet arrangements
  had begun
To bury them as they received their call.

The doctors raved and stormed as the gory total
  grew
The yellow bastards sneered at all they said
The bland reply was simple, the railway must go
  through
Even though the place was filled with British
  dead.

Then the rain began to fall, and the working
  party small
Had to work as coolies never worked before
And they had to walk for miles to the deeply cut
  defiles
Where the yellow swine forever drove them
  more.

They returned to camp at dark looking
  haggard, worn and stark
Their backs and aching shoulders fiery red

They were fed on jungle stew, then 'twas all they
  could do
To bring their weary bodies off the bed.

When they woke before the dawn, even hope had
  almost gone
But they thought of stricken comrades who had
  fell
So when daylight trickled through you could see
  the ragged crew
As they ploughed along the road to hell.

On a still and tropic night with a death rate at
  its height
The living aching suffering prayed to God
But no succour came until that God-forsaken
  rail went through
'Twas the vengeance of the little yellow god.

There's a camp of ghostly horrors to the north of
  Kanyu II
There are scores of bamboo crosses in the mud
There'll be broken-hearted women when the tale
  of it gets thro'
May the living God avenge with yellow blood.

Bob 'Buck' Taylor
The Royal Signals

Bob Taylor was born in Castle Bromwich in 1920. His father was an Australian Pilot in the Royal Flying Corps and his mother was German but of Danish extraction from Schleswig-Holstein. His father returned to Australia in 1922 and he never saw him again. He remained with his mother's family in Schleswig-Holstein (and went to Danish school) until 1938 when it became clear that war was imminent. He had been actively sought as a recruit by the Hitler Youth and his mother advised him to leave for England. He arrived in London as a merchant seaman and eventually joined the Royal Signals in October 1938. He became a wireless operator and was looking forward to a posting to India in October 1939 but the outbreak of war in September put a stop to that.

He was in the British Expeditionary Force in France as a dispatch rider until May 1940 when he was evacuated at Dunkirk. For the rest of the war he was attached to 1 Commando Brigade and landed on Sword Beach on D Day. He fought through France and Belgium, crossing the Maas, Rhine, Aller, Weser and Elbe before the end of the war. After the war he served with the Middlesex Yeomanry, was sent to Egypt, was with 11 Armoured Division and finally with 48th (TA) Signals Regiment, before being demobbed on 1960.

Following demobilisation, he returned to Germany as a boat builder in Schleswig-Holstein until 1978 and was then a crane driver until 1985. From then until early 2001 he acted as a water bailiff in Nord Friesland. Sadly, his wife died in 2001 when he applied to become a resident at the Royal Hospital. By his own admission he had a colourful career in the Army and has recounted a few of his escapades.

Miscellaneous Misdemeanours and Some Lucky Escapes
Bob 'Buck' Taylor

I remember we were at Rose Markie as part of a Beach Landing Party based near Inverness. This was in 1941 and a mate of mine had had an invitation to a dance. The problem was how to get there. So we made a plan, and on the night in question we pushed a jeep to the camp perimeter wire and cut a jeep-sized hole in the wire. We manhandled the jeep through the wire and at a safe distance 'hot-wired' the jeep and made our way to a very enjoyable party. On our return we reversed the process and stealthily pushed the jeep back through the wire. Someone must have suspected something for just as we were replacing the wire the perimeter lights came on and there we were, surrounded by armed sentries, caught in the act. Misuse of military property, criminal damage to War Office property, theft, absence, you name it, they dealt it! This cost us 14 days in the nick but as the whole regiment was away on exercise we had the camp to ourselves. I think we got away pretty lightly.

Christmas 1944 saw us in Holland and we thought a nice fat pig would do us nicely for Christmas dinner. We crept up to a farm and kidnapped this pig, wrapping a sandbag round its head to stifle its squealing. It was too heavy for me, however, and got away. Just as we started in pursuit there was a burst of machine gun fire and no more pig. We often wondered whether the Germans enjoyed 'our' pig but were thankful to have got away with nothing more than a severe fright.

I was taken prisoner for an hour or so in Belgium in 1940. I had been sent to contact 9th Guards Brigade at Furnes in Belgium, about 50 miles from Dunkirk. I was a Despatch Rider at the time. It was a long drive on an Army motorcycle and the situation was chaotic, with refugees, soldiers and the Lord knows what else on the roads and I had to stop and rest. I had not been asleep for long when I was roused by a grunted command in German, a language I have spoken since childhood. Covered by a machine pistol I was made to get up by this German and we marched off leaving the motorbike by the side of the road. After a couple of hundred yards I pretended to have stomach-ache and diarrhoea and he gestured to an empty farmhouse. 'Get in there and do you business,' he ordered. I needed no second bidding and was into the house like a rabbit, slamming doors behind me as I went before diving out of a back window and sprinting across the yard and into the arms of the South Lancashires.

I was driving Brigadier Derek Mills-Roberts, the Commander of 1st Commando Brigade on a reconnaissance in 1944 and after a while I stopped the jeep as I was sure we were lost. The Brigadier's language was far worse than any soldier's and he disagreed with me but told me to clamber up a bocage bank and have a look-see. In the field was a German Nebelwerfer (multi-barrelled rocked launcher) and what seemed to be about half the German Army round it. I hurriedly retreated and told the Brigadier. 'No problems', he said. 'We'll take them out'. I pointed out that we had a Thompson sub-machine gun and a Colt .45 revolver and that the odds were pretty heavily stacked against us. Eventually he agreed and we lit out pretty quickly. Just round the corner, and directly in our path was a Volkswagen staff car with a couple of Germans standing by it. We gritted our teeth and with me firing the Thompson with one hand and steering with the other and the Brigadier loosing off with his revolver we managed to skid round the Germans and back on the road to safety.

I landed at Ouistreham at 0800 on D Day (6th June 1944) and the following day was sent as part of an armoured OP to 33 Field Regiment (oddly enough the same unit that I had been with when we had misappropriated the Jeep in Scotland). In my Bren Carrier was the CO of 33 Field Regiment and his Adjutant and in the following vehicle was the G3 of 7 Brigade. We must have been under observation because before we knew it we were under fire. I think it must have been Panzerfausts (hand-held anti-tank grenade launchers) as both vehicles were hit and they were throwing grenades as well. I can remember the Adjutant being thrown out in front of me. I was hit in the head and legs by shrapnel and staggered from the Bren Carrier to the safety of some nearby buildings. Before I knew it I had fallen into a cess pit (some poetic justice there maybe!) and was eventually dragged out before being sent off to the nearest aid post where they almost died of the smell. They bandaged me up and before long I had rejoined my unit – another lucky escape.

Dougie Wright MM
Special Air Service

Dougie Wright has never been one for the quiet life. He was born near Macclesfield in 1919 and set his sights on joining the police force in Stockport. He was advised to join the Guards for three years as a way of guaranteeing his entry into the police and duly enlisted into the Grenadier Guards at the end of 1938. In the end, of course, Herr Hitler upset his plans and he never did get into the police.

After basic training at the Guards Depot he joined the King's Company, 1st Battalion Grenadier Guards at Chelsea Barracks, before moving to France as part of the British Expeditionary Force. He was actively involved at Dunkirk, where the battalion acted as rearguard, and was fortunate, together with a dozen other men, to find a rowing boat in which they made their way to a larger ship, were hoist on board and after a meal of cocoa and bully beef, fell into exhausted sleep. They woke to the sound of shouting and found the entire upper deck was crammed with soldiers cheering the White Cliffs of Dover. During their trip the ship had been dive-bombed and lost half its bridge together with several crew, but they had slept right through all that.

After a period in England Dougie joined the 6th Battalion and moved to North Africa as part of 201 Guards Brigade. Not long afterwards he volunteered for the Special Air Service and then joined the Special Boat Service under Lord Jellicoe. They carried out raids in Sardinia, Crete and Yugoslavia and he won the MM on a raid on the island of Amorgos.

In 1946 he was medically discharged and spent the next ten years farming in Cheshire, before re-joining the Grenadiers and becoming the Pioneer Sergeant in Malta, Cyprus and the Guards Training Battalion at Pirbright, after which he was posted to the 3rd battalion as Police Sergeant. The next few years saw postings as varied as Tidworth, the Cameroons and Chelsea, before he became a butcher at the Guards Depot, Hubbelrath and later Wuppertal. He went on a United Nations tour in Cyprus in 1965 and to Sharjah in the Persian Gulf in 1969, before finally being discharged in 1970.

Dougie took up a variety of occupations as butcher, security guard and in the Prison Service before finally retiring in 1984. He joined the ranks of the Royal Hospital for the first time in 1995, but missed the life outside and transferred to out-pension a couple of years later. However, he changed his mind and donned scarlet again in 1998. Dougie is a firm supporter of the In-Pensioners club and in his spare time cultivates his allotment. His great regret is that the Royal Hospital does not keep pigs, which he reckons would do well on the swill from the Great Kitchen. As a butcher, he should know.

He has recounted for us a couple of his many adventures.

No Answer Came the Strange Reply
Dougie Wright

About the end of April 1944 our patrol of ten men embarked on M.L. (Motor Launch) 1398 from our base in Turkish waters and landed on the island of Naxos. The following morning it was reported to us that five Germans were manning a wireless station and our orders were to capture or destroy it. We lay up in a large shepherd's compound made of dry stone wall and were soon in contact with the Greeks who were able to give us some valuable local intelligence.

The German in charge of the wireless station was said to be a 'SS' man and we learned that there were two men on duty at night with three off. Two of them used to go to the local wine bar while the SS man had a lady friend whom he slept with each night. We decided to attack the next night and split into three groups. When the wine bar closed we laid in wait for the two chaps whom we captured. The two on duty resisted and were killed. The SS man, a sergeant, was literally caught with his pants down. Was he angry! He said he would never have been captured alive if we hadn't caught him unarmed, and declared he would escape at the earliest opportunity. Every five minutes he would stand up, give a Nazi salute and shout 'Heil Hitler'. He was a fine figure of a man but completely brainwashed.

The following day our wireless operator, Viv, received a message saying we would be picked up that night by M.L. 1398, proceed to sea and join forces with M.L. 1380 who had on board another patrol 'mostly from the Greek Sacred Squadron' to go on another raid on the island of Amorgos.

We left Naxos about midnight into a rough sea. I always got sea-sick on these boats and got permission to stay on deck and man a twin Lewis gun. It was a wild night with heavy seas – ideal for our sort of work –and just as first light was breaking the lookout reported 'ship on the port bow'. E Boats were operating in these waters, so we flashed the code signal in Morse. No reply. We repeated the signal three times and received no answer. By now I had my sights firmly on the black blob in the water 500 yards away, apparently at a standstill. We were soon at full speed, travelling anti-clockwise to the other boat, the captured SS man down below was cheering and making a tremendous din. He had evidently understood the words 'E Boat' and one of them would have finished us. We were on full standby and very alert.

The Captain ordered us to open fire which we did with oerlikon and machine guns and soon we could see smoke pouring from the aft of the other boat. I concentrated my fire on and just above the water line and must have loosed off at least a couple of hundred rounds. Daylight was approaching and to my dismay the outline of the other boat took a distinct resemblance to the M.L. we were to meet. I shouted to the Captain who immediately ordered us to cease fire. Not a shot had been returned at us. We closed on the other boat and discovered that three men were wounded and that she was taking in water. We made it to a small barren island where we camouflaged ourselves and had a council of war to find out what had gone wrong. The Captains had two different codes, one for the Mediterranean and one for the Aegean.

It was decided that our M.L. would take both patrols to mount the raid on Amorgos. The other would try to make it to Castel-crosso with the prisoners. Captain Clarke MC and I had done a recce of this island the previous year to find an airstrip and capture the only German on the island. The ten Germans now on the island had taken over the village school, but we knew the lie of the land. I positioned myself on a flat-topped roof to give covering fire with the rest of the patrol behind a wall on the other side of the school. At the given signal I fired ten Bren gun magazines, loaded with a good mixture of Ball, Tracer, Incendiary and Armour Piercing ammunition raking all the windows and doors of the building. Nine Germans were killed and we captured some valuable documents.

Some six months later, whilst on our way to capture Salonika we lay up on the island of Amorgos. During the daytime I went ashore to exchange some tinned food for fresh lamb and met up with a shepherd boy who got very excited and said there were three British soldiers living in his village. They had come ashore in a dinghy and were wounded. Unfortunately I could not stay any longer but I discovered afterwards that these were the three wounded matelots from M.L. 1380 which was officially reported 'sunk at sea'. I have always felt responsible for the sinking of one of His Majesty's ships.

Peter Carrie
*The Royal Armoured Corps
and The Royal Air Force*

Joining the Kings Own Scottish Borderers in 1934 at 19, Pete, with the mechanical experience gained in his father's haulage business, volunteered for the Royal Tank Corps and trained at their Depot at Bovingdon.

Drafted to India a year later he became a member of the 7th Light Tank Company at Cawnpore. In 1936 they were equipped with Crossley Armoured Cars and two years later with the rank of Lance Corporal (unpaid) he became a Driver Mechanic.

Duties consisted of supporting the civil authorities in Lucknow, Calcutta and Patra, later moving up to the N.W. Frontier to relieve 10 Light Tank Company where they patrolled the border in MK4 and MK5 Light Tanks carrying LMGs, and powered by Rolls Royce or Meadows engines.

Shortly before the outbreak of war, he returned to the UK to train reservists and officers at Catterick on Matilda MK1 and

MK2 tanks, and then with two stripes he joined the BEF, travelling to Brussels. During this intensive period of delaying tactics to prevent the German advance, his regiment succeeded in ambushing the enemy's leading mobile column, but eventually fell back to Arras, and then leapfrogged to Dunkirk. They arrived with only two tanks remaining. Pete in the meantime had been wounded, and to make it even worse he was shot in both legs by an ME110 as he lay on the boat taking him to England. Obviously a long period in hospital followed at Leatherhead, and then his old stamping ground at Catterick, before medical discharge in 1940 and treatment for almost 3 years afterwards.

In 1943, failing to get back into the Army on medical grounds, he persuaded the RAFVR to take him, and before long, with his mechanical experience, he was posted to RAF Blyton near Ely as a Flight Engineer, and with three stripes, and instead of the confines of a tank, it was into the open skies as a Lancaster crew member and bombing raids over Germany with 43 (NZ) Squadron.

In 1946 he was finally discharged, again on medical grounds, and joined his father-in-law's company in Manchester till 1968, retiring to enjoy the Maltese sun after the death of his wife in 1969, and thence to Andorra with his niece and family, until 1996 – when he donned his third, and possibly most colourful uniform, the Chelsea Scarlet.

Tanks for the Memory!
Pete Carrie

Not such a corny title as you may think, because my military career has been mainly spent with some sort of armoured vehicle or another, and so my memories are very much involved with them.

In these days of technology, satellites and guided missiles, it is amazing when I look back and think of my first vehicles on the North West Frontier in 1936. These were in fact already twelve years old when we got them; Crossley armoured cars with solid tyres which didn't make for easy riding. So-called modernisation came when we lifted off the existing bodies and fitted them to Chevrolets which had been specially built in Canada. With these new vehicles, we patrolled our section of the road through the N.W. Frontier engaged from time to time in the odd skirmish with the tribesmen, in order to keep the route open.

Skirmishes of course came in different sizes, from a small outbreak of fighting and shooting, to maybe a full scale attack when perhaps we faced something like 2,000 or more all surrounding our outpost. At these times, we had with us Sikhs and Gurkhas, and I can assure you that there is nothing more blood-curdling or terrifying than to hear the Sikhs' war cry as they go into battle, and always with devastating results for the enemy.

After a while it was decided that we would pull back from the area, and that our vehicles would he handed over to the Indian TA in Calcutta, and that we should deliver them. So began what I can only call an armoured tourist trail – travelling over 1500 miles. As it happened my brother was in the party, and for the first part of the journey, we travelled by local train from Kohat, where we settled into the best carriage behind the engine. Suddenly the train came to a halt, and, thinking we had been ambushed, we kept our revolvers at the ready, only to find an apparently injured camel lying across the track. My brother, deciding to put it out of its misery was just about to fire, when up it got and ambled off into the desert!

The rest of the journey passed without incident, and we eventually reached Rawalpindi, and knowing we could mess with the RAF, hailed a taxi. However, as there were six of us we couldn't all get in, whereupon the taxi driver offered the wheel to my brother and we set off with the driver running behind. He eventually caught us up at the camp and was paid. Can you imagine a cabbie doing that here?

Next day we collected our vehicles and set off down the famous Great North Road to Calcutta. Along this highway are a series of Dak bungalows, built as stopovers for officers with accommodation, food etc., so nothing ventured, nothing gained, and despite our lower ranks, we took advantage of them, and also refuelled at local barracks en route. As this journey took many weeks we took advantage of the freedom that our situation offered, and amongst the adventures we had I can remember was our visit to Amritsar to have a dekko at the famous Golden Temple. Here we were in luck as our Sikh electrician was related to one of the officials; so, donning golden turbans and removing our shoes we were given a VIP tour and also went home with him for a meal with his family. At Cawnpore, being broke, we flogged the petrol from one of the armoured cars to a local taxi driver, and then, towing the fuelless vehicle set off to Agra to see the Taj Mahal. Arriving to find it closed, we banged on the gates, whereupon the caretaker, seeing two armoured cars with turrets pointing at him surrendered, and not only opened the gates, but gave us a complete tour of the place, including climbing the minarets from which we got amazing views of the tomb below, and also the surrounding countryside.

Gates of a different sort were opened at Delhi, for having decided to have a shufti at the city, and New Delhi in particular, we set off down the ceremonial King's Way, through the War memorial Arch right up to the Vice Regal buildings, really I suppose the equivalent of driving through Admiralty Arch, down a closed Mall to the gates of Buckingham Palace.

However, here without any hesitation, seeing two armoured cars approaching, the Bengal Lancers swung open the gates, and in we drove, had a good look round and set off back down the King's Way. We gathered that there was a huge stink trying to discover what unit had had the cheek to do this, but by then we were miles away, and I think the poor old Tank Corps got the blame.

Whilst we were in barracks at Delhi, the Royal Tank Corps was transferred into the Royal Armoured Corps, and so there was a huge celebratory pissup when all the funds from the PRI were blown in one evening with two or more days, as you can imagine, for recovery afterwards.

However, we did complete our task, and eventually returned to camp, and from then onwards, soldiering became very much more serious, but I am grateful for the opportunity it gave me to see some of India in the last historic days of the Raj – even though I was still an unpaid Lance Corporal.

My life from then onwards changed dramatically, and painfully, and after medical discharge, a time at home till 1943, I managed to get back into uniform again, but this time with the boys in blue as a Flight Engineer in the RAF flying Lancasters. Life, of course, was totally different to that I had experienced in the army, and so was the action. Whereas on the ground you met your opponent face to face, thousands of feet in the air things were so much more impersonal, though the flak and fighter attacks were rather hairy.

We were lucky in that we were the second lot to get Radar in the RAF which was an enormous help. Before then we relied on the pathfinder 'Mozzies' which used to go in ahead of us and drop green marker flares. However, Jerry cottoned on to this, and so lit green flares off target to confuse us. We then used red ones which again they copied, so at times it became bloody confusing with instructions coming from all sides to 'bomb green and bomb red'; thus we were sometimes over the target for over an hour trying to sort it out and being shot at like hell and using up valuable fuel.

We used to drop 'window' in huge amounts; this was metallic strips that as they floated down confused the enemy radar. However, the only trouble was that by the time we had dropped it, Jerry had plotted our speed ahead and so gave us a real pasting with flak and fighters.

Loss of aircraft and buddies was always sad, and could be dangerous too. Once our Squadron Leader, flying ahead of us with his bomb doors open, received a direct hit and blew up in our face, and we found ourselves flying through the flaming debris and remains of the aircraft. We then took the lead. Some bombs were so enormous that the bomb doors could not be closed, so you can imagine what it felt like flying with that beneath you, and also how the aircraft shot upwards once all this weight had been released.

Air miles and destinations were a little different in those days, but like my Indian and other experiences, I'm proud to have taken part in them, and fortunate to have survived to remember them.

Alf Amphlett BEM
REME

Enlisting in the Worcestershire Regiment (TA) as a Junior Musician (Fife) at the age of 15 in 1937, two years later he was embodied into the TA, and in October 1939 found himself transferred to the RA stationed in Brighton, London, and later Essex with 70 SL Regiment.

In 1942 he mustered as a Vehicle Fitter, and in 1944 was compulsorily transferred to the RASC at Glasgow, moving with the unit to N.W. Europe after the Arromanches landing in June of that year.

Then followed the familiar and fought over route to Caen, Wesel, the Rhine Crossing, and finally into Denmark for the German surrender, and a return home and demob in August 1946.

Ten months later at Norwich, he re-enlisted and after a spell with RASC at Thetford was posted to Germany and 980 Car Company RASC at Bielefeld, moving with them to Hamburg. By May 1949 he was an Acting Mechanist S/Sgt. and in July 1951 returned to the UK and Colchester to join 21 Company RASC, but transferred to REME as part of the 'pulling together' of that Corps.

Following an Armament Artificer Vehicle course, he was posted to 25 Field Engineer Regiment LAD in the Middle East, as an A/ASM in 1954, returning with them to the UK a year later.

Things hotted up in more ways than one when in 1956 he was picked to go as the REME Support with a detachment of 50 personnel from 25 Field Engineer Regiment to the Montebello Islands in the South Pacific for the famous 'Bomb' tests of that name, and was awarded the BEM for his work as Base Engineer maintaining vehicles and plant during the tests.

This experience undoubtedly played a part in his selection in November 1956 to go as a member of the Antarctic Expedition for the International Geophysical Year run by the Royal Society. With this he remained in the Antarctic for 2 years responsible as Base Engineer for the installing of generators, maintaining vehicles, etc. Back from the snowy wastes in 1959 he went to REME Technical Wing FVRDE at Chobham where he was discharged in March 1963 sporting with his ribbons that of the Polar Medal awarded for his work in Antarctica. This discharge was before the end of his engagement because he had been offered another trip to the Antarctic where he spent just over 12 months looking after generators and dogs.

1965 saw him back again at Halley Bay, the permanent base of the British Antarctic Society, the rigours of which can be judged by the loss of three people in a crevasse.

His obvious scientific skills continued to be used in civilian employment, and for 17 years he worked as a Science Laboratory Technician in various schools. Early musical skills have not been forgotten either, for at the Royal Hospital which he joined in 1988, he can be heard playing the flute with the Royal Hospital Band and Chelsea College Wind Orchestra.

'Never refuse anything that's offered'
Alf Amphlett

So said my father, and indeed that is a philosophy that I have followed, and which resulted in my involvement in the following events, all totally different from my previous military experiences.

In December 1955, HMS Narvik, a converted L.S.T. taken out of mothballs, steamed out of Portsmouth heading for the Montebello Islands in the South Pacific to take part in two atomic tests christened 'Operation Mosaic'. With my REME experience I had been selected to go as one of the Maintenance team responsible for the upkeep of the various items of mechanical and electrical gear essential to the operation's success.

As you can imagine, there was a massive amount of work to be done in preparation for the tests; the establishing of a base, accommodation, roads, runways, even bathing pools. All this needed equipment such as generators, bulldozers, cranes, etc., and all needing care and maintenance, and whilst the Sappers did the construction work itself, it was our job to see that everything was kept running. Our team consisted of myself as Staff Sgt., one vehicle mechanic and one M.T. Fitter, and to this was added a Corporal who had plant experience, and a M.T. NCO.

The equipment was not new, but reconditioned did not live up to expectations, and within days 'nonsenses' were occurring and the 'black gang' as we were called, worked day and night to keep it all going. Spares were flown in from Perth, but it often came down to 'make do and mend' with us stripping down bulldozers, welding selectors in gear boxes and making new bearings, often within 24 hours.

With plant so widely scattered, our team should have been much larger. For instance the distance from the ship to the control hut on South Hermite took one and a half hours, whilst to the two target areas took twenty to thirty minutes. However, by dint of working flat out for up to three or four days without sleep, we managed to keep on top of things. Weather played an important part, and as it turned out, from April 7th until the end of June, there were only two days good enough for firing, but thanks to everyone's efforts we were able to use both of them.

Weapon towers were erected for the actual firing and two camera towers, not an easy task in the high winds of April, plus having to cope with inaccuracies in the manufacture of the various sections which proved a nuisance, especially at such heights.

Overseeing the power winches, and gear

involved in all this work was very demanding as well as maintaining other plant such as the fifteen generators and vehicles, etc.

The actual hoisting of the weapons into the towers for firing was a very nail biting experience. Weighing 10 tons, and slowly inched into position by a winch on a D7 Caterpillar, one could not risk any movement or drop due to a slipped clutch. I operated the winch on the D7 tractor – an awesome task under the tense and watchful eyes of the scientists.

Once aloft we retired to 'safety' for the first test to a nearby island where we sat in a hollow and felt the heat of the explosion and fireball on our backs. For the second one, 24 hours later, we actually went into a shelter. Both were daytime firings so not nearly as visually dramatic as it would have been at night.

After the explosions, recce parties suitably clothed went ashore to gather instruments and data, and we began packing up. So quickly was this done that within a week the islands were deserted, apart from a stripped down camera tower and the tell tale radio active dust in the stratosphere.

HMS Narvik raised anchor and set sail, but not home by the usual route, for as we reached Aden the Suez crisis broke out and we were directed round the Cape. All in all a fascinating experience, and as I said earlier, so different from the activities one would normally be involved in, with the added bonus of a BEM ribbon on my tunic.

An 'offer' of another sort came in November 1956 when I was seconded to the Royal Society International Geophysical Year Antarctic Expedition to Halley Bay as Senior Diesel Mechanic. We sailed from Butler's Wharf, being seen off by HM The Queen, and in company with Dr. Vivian Fuchs and members of the Trans-Antarctic Expedition to Shackleton Base.

En route we called at Madeira and Montevideo and South Georgia entering the ice pack on December 23rd; a little different from the heat of the South Pacific. By December 30th we were stuck in the ice and on the first occasion it took us over 5 hours to free ourselves, and the second a further 4 hours.

We eventually made it to Halley by January 3rd 1957, and remained there for just over two years. As in Operation Mosaic, my responsibility was the maintenance of generators, snow cats and other gear, but in far different and more difficult conditions.

During this time the scientists carried out their observations, meteorology, radio astronomy, geomagnetics etc., and looking back now my photographs resemble very much those of the earlier Antarctic expeditions with huskies, penguins and the inevitable beards very much to the fore. Our conditions were obviously better, and we did get supply ships and the odd helicopter arriving. Our eventual return to the UK was delayed by a five-day imprisonment in the ice from which we only escaped by the use of explosive charges on poles inserted down the side of the ship to loosen the ice.

In 1961 I learnt that my ribbons were to be extended yet again by the award of the Polar Medal for my services, which as with Operation Mosaic, was an experience in the course of duty which I normally could not expect to have had in an army career.

My father's advice was to be taken yet again, for prior to my release in 1963, I was 'offered' another trip to the Antarctic for 12 months to Signy Island looking after generators and dogs, and two years later a return to my old haunts at Halley Bay, now a permanent British base – so all I can say is, listen to your father!

Charlie Hutchison
Special Air Service

Born during World War I at Perth in 1916, it was at the age of 18 that Charlie enlisted in the Argyll and Sutherland Highlanders (TA) at Stirling. Four months later he signed on as a regular, and by 1936 was en route to India with the 2nd Battalion.

Echoes of boys' adventure stories followed, with a spell on the North West Frontier before posting to Singapore which he fortunately left in 1940 to join the 1st Battalion in Palestine and Egypt.

There things hotted up, and he was sent to Crete and was lucky enough to escape by destroyer to Egypt. His platoon acted as bodyguard to General Montgomery before the battle of El Alamein in 1942 and they were certainly in the thick of it. After this he switched opponents and location to Eritrea to tackle the Italians; this lasted until 1943 when, like so many, he was shipped back to the UK to prepare for D Day.

Landing in Normandy with the 7th Battalion as part of the famous 51st Highland Division, the force pushed forward across N.W. Europe. Unfortunately, Charlie's progress came to a painful halt in the Reichsfeldt Forest in Holland where he received a 'Blighty' wound in the chest – straight through his regimental tattoo. Returned to England and hospital for treatment he was eventually discharged in 1946.

However, it was only three months before he talked himself back into uniform and out to Jerusalem with the 1st Battalion getting his 'knees brown' until 1948 when they returned home to Colchester, and the following year embarked yet again, this time for Hong Kong and the New Territories where he was involved in the campaign in the jungles of Malaysia against the terrorists. With this experience, when the conflict started in Korea the Battalion was an obvious choice, and so aboard HMS Belfast in company with assorted livestock such as sheep, chickens and pigs, they arrived at Seoul and took up position on the front line, with all that this implies. The end of hostilities saw repatriation by the USAF, and in April 1952 a return to Hong Kong followed by Edinburgh and his transfer to the SAS.

Proof of his fitness for this role was the passing of the arduous Brecon course at the age of 37, and 14 years after he first arrived in Singapore, he was back there again, this time with 22 SAS for patrol duties.

Clocking up even more miles he returned to Stirling in 1955 to rejoin the Argylls, but before long the SAS were calling, and it was back south to train 23 SAS and a third spell in Singapore in 1958 with a final posting to the Persian Gulf before returning home to the sedate surroundings of Malvern where he was discharged after 26 years with the colours.

Civilian life, until he joined the Royal Hospital in 1996, included work as a long distance lorry driver, the hotel trade and London Transport.

Ye Canna Cawcanny

You will always remember the 10th of December
The morning broke cold, bright and clear,
As the Argyll's drove from their chilly repose
They were shelled from the front, flank and rear.
Now the shells from the flank took the toll

of the ranks
As the Argyll's goal was in sight;
But at every fixed line they left many
behind,
And some who were far beyond aid.
Of our amoured might they were nowhere
in sight
Our artillery was some other where
But on that fateful day the Argylls held
sway
As they stormed the heights of Barrani,
Now the Ities they know as they were the
foe
With a Scotsman – Ye canna cawcanny.
By Charlie Hutchinson, Sidi Barram 1942

A Few Random Shots...
Charlie Hutchison

I think you have caught me just in time,
because, like the title of the book my
memories are beginning to fade. However,
during my twenty six years in uniform there
are one or two stories that still come to
mind and may be of interest, or amuse you.

I suppose the funniest, though not for me,
was during my spell with General Montgomery in the Western Desert before El Alamein.

Our platoon had been appointed as his bodyguard and went everywhere with him.

As you all know, he was pretty strict, and this particularly applied to smoking, which was forbidden. However, we used to find opportunities when we could have a quick drag without his knowing.

Such an opportunity occurred for me late one night when we were bivouacked in the desert and Monty was in his pit in the famous caravan. I settled down on the steps of the vehicle and lit up; imagine my horror as I heard the door open behind me. Fearing he had smelt the tobacco I stubbed out my fag and sat still in the total darkness.

No clipped tones of accusation and reprimand followed. Instead I felt a warm flow over my head and shoulders as the General answered a call of nature, unaware of me crouching below him in the darkness. I dared not move, and finally when he had finished, I escaped, wondering if I am the only man to he treated so by a future Field Marshal?

I did, however, get my revenge a little later on at Christmas when I found that the cook had produced a Christmas 'duff' (pudding) for Monty. This, I confess, I stole and gave to the lads to enjoy instead. As it may have had alcohol in it perhaps he wouldn't have enjoyed it anyway!

Another tale with perhaps more sinister lavatorial connections occurred during the Korean War in 1951, when we were holding the line against the Chinese. Each morning an old peasant woman would appear near our position to relieve herself, bringing with her a spade which she stuck in the ground before burying the result. However, after she departed we underwent a huge 'stonking' from the Chinese and this became a regular occurrence, so much so that our Colonel became highly suspicious. One day with the help of a machine gun or two we made sure that this was her last appearance, and our suspicions proved to be correct, for the spade she dug into the ground concealed an aerial with which she was transmitting to the Chinese, from then onwards the bombardment ceased, at that time anyway.

Those of you who used to watch M.A.S.H. may get a little idea of how life was like in Korea. On our arrival, we were chuffed to be kitted out in American gear which was very practical and warm. However, the powers that be frowned on this, and before long we were back in ill-fitting battledresses and so cold that our boots froze to our feet. Another memory of those days was the actual fighting for various positions on the front. These would be captured, overrun and recaptured so often in fact that we used to leave our machine guns behind, but just take the bolts with us. The Chinese never touched them as they were useless unless fitted with the bolts, which we, of course, took back with us to fire on the Chinese again – war is strange at times!

Strange too are the echoes and reminders one gets years after an event. During the Ardennes campaign I gave up my leave entitlement so a buddy could go home to break the news to his mother that his brother had been killed. My reward for this action was to be shot a few days later, not only through the chest, but also through my regimental tattoo, seemingly by two bullets, With such a wound I could not fly by aircraft due to the atmospheric pressure, and so it was not until six weeks later that I hoarded a hospital plane that flew me to blighty, at 500 feet, to avoid any trouble.

Years later, married and on holiday, I one day felt a sharp pain down my left side, and there surfacing, and later dug out after all those years, and a journey round my body, was my souvenir of the Ardennes!

Charlie Boyce DCM
The Reconnaissance Corps

Charlie Boyce is a Brummie, born in the Ladywood district of the city 1915. He left school at 14 and went to work as a grocer's assistant until he was called up in April 1940. He was posted initially to the 2nd Monmouthshires, a TA Infantry battalion, and after recruit training joined the brigade anti-tank company. In early 1941 the three anti-tank companies of the 53rd Welsh Division were used to form 53 Reconnaissance Regiment. Although somewhat stooped now, Charlie then was an impressive looking chap, standing a good 6'2" and with the barrel chest of the champion swimmer he was before the war. Perhaps unsurprisingly his nickname in the Recce Corps was 'Tiny'! He made Sergeant in nine months and for the next three years he and his unit were engaged in exhaustive training all over the UK.

53 Recce Regiment landed in Normandy in the summer of 1944 in the dismounted role, relieving the Ox and Bucks. Charlie

was Troop Sergeant and after the battle for Caen they reverted to their primary recce role in their Humber armoured cars and Bren carriers with their 6 pounder anti-tank guns. They were involved in the operations to close the Falaise Gap to encircle the retreating German armies and linked up with the Americans. His four anti-tank guns were in action supported by the Vickers heavy machine guns of the Manchesters and around 8000 Germans surrendered in the operation. He recalls well a three-hour period during this time when they were shelled by their own artillery, came under fire from German 88s and were attacked by rocket-carrying Typhoon ground attack aircraft, all fortunately without a scratch.

After this, the armour was reformed, with recce leading, leapfrogging forward fighting tough little battles with isolated but determined enemy rearguard pockets until they reached and liberated Lille in northern France. There followed the dash to Antwerp and through Belgium and into Holland, relieving Eindhoven where the grateful workers at the Philips electronics factory presented them with the smallest radios they had ever seen for listening to the news. They liberated s'Hertogenbosch and were engaged in flank protection during the Arnhem operation after which they were withdrawn to the Ardennes region where they spent a cold and uncomfortable period during the hardest winter seen for years, when the Germans attempted a breakthrough at the well known 'Battle of the Bulge'.

They crossed the Rhine successfully in late March '45 and a month later Charlie won his immediate DCM. At the end of the war the regiment found itself at Hamburg. They were amalgamated briefly with the North Irish Horse and finally returned home in early 1946.

Charlie nearly stayed in the Army, but decided to get married instead and after a few years with Rover in Birmingham and at a petroleum depot near Maidstone, he joined the Prison Service and saw service in Maidstone, Parkhurst and Oxford prisons before retiring in 1975.

Charlie joined the Royal Hospital in 2002 and straight away got stuck into his allotment. Unfortunately, the years have taken their toll and Charlie is now resigned to being a permanent resident in the Infirmary.

Caen to Hamburg
Charlie Boyce

Because his memory is not what it was Charlie has agreed, albeit reluctantly, to the inclusion of the citation for his Distinguished Conduct Medal as his contribution to these memoirs.

The London Gazette 2nd August 1945
'On 27th April 1945 a Troop of 'C' Squadron had received orders to seize the bridge at Kulverborstel. This troop was supported by a section of anti-tank guns commanded by Sergeant Boyce. On arriving at a bend in the road about 800 yards from the bridge, at a point where the road turned to run parallel with the river, the leading car came under observed mortar and Spandau fire from a position on a rise on the far side of the river. The armoured cars deployed to their right and returned the enemy fire. Sergeant Boyce also deployed the leading gun and, still under fire from the opposite bank of the river gave the crew orders for action. When this gun was engaging the enemy with H.E., Sergeant Boyce returned to his second gun and found that the number one and the loader had both been badly wounded in the legs and were

unable to get their gun into action. He hastily made a reconnaissance for a suitable position and, replacing the wounded men with others from his headquarter detachment, got the gun into action. The flat and open ground to the right of the road was the only place where the guns could be got into action quickly. This meant that the operation would have to be carried out for some distance in full view of the enemy. This whole area was consequently subjected to continual mortar and machine gun fire from the enemy position on the opposite bank. When satisfied that his guns were effectively engaging the enemy, Sergeant Boyce in full view of the enemy ran to the wounded men and after applying field dressings placed one of the men, whom he realised had a broken leg, on a gate which he found nearby and dragged him back for a distance of 300 yards. He then returned to the second man and as he also had a fractured leg placed him on the gate and dragged him back to safety.

Sergeant Boyce's actions no doubt saved the lives of his two men, while he effectively maintained his section of guns in action against the enemy. This contributed largely towards the success of the Troop operation in which the bridge was captured and held.'

Robert Crabb BEM
The Scots Guards

Robert Crabb was born in 1921 in Murthly, Perthshire where his father was under-gamekeeper to the Lyle estate. He was the eldest of nine children, having 5 brothers and 3 sisters. His first schoolteacher was a Miss Ballantyne, whose record of a 64 pound salmon killed on the Tay still stands. He was educated locally until the age of 16 when his father decreed that he should join the Scots Guards as a piper in the steps of the legendary Alec Macdonald.

Robert enlisted at Caterham in January 1938 as a boy of 16. He had started playing the pipes at the age of 6, but had to unlearn most what he had been taught at home. He was sent to the first battalion in 1939, but when war broke out all those under age were removed from the war service battalions and Robert spent most of the war years in the UK on a variety of garrison and other duties.

Just before the end of the war he was posted to the second battalion which had reached Belgium and from there entered Germany. They spent a few days at the town of Stade on the Elbe river near Hamburg and thereafter were sent to Cuxhaven from where the surrender of Heligoland was mounted. From there, he was attached as a Lance Corporal piper to Left Flank who were to form the British contingent at the Potsdam Conference where they spent a month.

He spent the next 18 years with the second battalion with postings to Germany and Malaya and rising to WO2 Pipe Major. He took the Pipe Band and Dancers all over the world – to the Calgary Stampede, Madison Square Gardens, the Alamo (where he played a lament for Davy Crockett), Moscow, Budapest, Hong Kong, Tunis and Cyprus, among other places and, of course, playing either individually or with the Pipe Band on every major State occasion before completing his engagement in 1962.

He had enjoyed close contacts with the City of London Police and through them, he became Usher to the Central Criminal Court, rising after 24 years to the post of Chief Jury Bailiff. Among the more notorious characters whom he dealt with were the Kray twins, John Profumo, James Hanratty and Rachman. He was at the same time Beadle of the Bread Street Ward. He retired in 1986 and was then beset by various health problems. His wife, whom he had married in 1941, died in 2004 and he entered a retirement home in Bermondsey, from which he was rescued, arriving at the Royal Hospital in August 2006.

Robert was awarded the British Empire Medal in 1954 for services to piping, including compiling the Scots Guards pipe manual of over 600 tunes, all of which he could play from memory. He was made a Queen's piper in 1954.

A Little Slice of History
Robert Crabb

It was a Sunday morning in June 1944. I was a member of the Pipe Band at the mounting of King's Guard at Buckingham Palace. We had just entered St James' Palace with the New Guard when we heard the engine note of a Doodle Bug. Then it cut out as it glided to its target. There was a terrific explosion and we were almost blown off our feet by the blast which we reckoned came from St James's Park.

Bye and bye we marched back to Buckingham Palace and from there played the Old Guard back to Wellington Barracks. As we approached the gate the Sergeant of the Guard was making unmistakable signs for us to 'double'. We ran into the barracks to be confronted by the dreadful sight of the Guards Chapel a huge pile of smouldering rubble. It had received a direct hit in the middle of Matins and there were 121 dead and 141 badly injured. The Pipe band's secondary function is always to act as stretcher bearers and pretty soon we were hard at work. It took us several days to recover the dead.

Following the German Surrender in May 1945 Right Flank Company with me as piper was selected to accompany the bigwigs to take the surrender of Heligoland. We left Cuxhaven on three German R boats, manned by German crews and I remember the Company Commander, Major Raeburn had two sentries with fixed bayonets posted in the engine room of each boat to stop any monkey business. No wonder he became a General! On the way to Cuxhaven by road from Stade we had heard that the road had been mined by German engineers. They had dug in these bloody great naval mines to try and catch a tank or two. So we got the German Engineer commander and his number two and stuck him on the leading tank to show the way through. We never hit anything but I don't know if that was because of him or just good luck. I have a photo of him on the tank just about to set off down the road and he doesn't look at all happy!

Just before all this I happened to notice a German ambulance by the side of the road one day. The keys were still in it and I though 'spoils of war' and all that, climbed in and drove off. Everyone thought it a great joke, including the Commanding Officer and the Divisional Commander and the Corps Commander and the rest, and even more so when it was discovered that I had 'liberated' the German area command vehicle full of radios and maps and whatnot masquerading as an ambulance.

I piped the Company ashore at Heligoland but for the rest of the time we were just an armed presence in case of trouble. The whole place had been blown apart by allied bombing which had tried to destroy the submarine pens. These were too well protected and scarcely damaged at all. It was amazing to see the damage on the outside, while inside there was a network of offices, stores, power stations and hospitals completely untouched. There was all sorts of stuff – beer, wine, tinned fruit, cameras, shotguns, delicacies of all kinds and we were told to help ourselves to whatever we wanted as the whole place was going to be blown up later. As you can imagine the Quartermaster had a field day! I collected half a dozen Lugers, but threw them into the sea later. I recall seeing a stretcher lying on the ground covered with a blanket. It didn't look as if there was anything in it but when I removed the blanket there was this thin old man with a wooden leg. I dug a shallow grave for him and tipped him in. I still have the stench of rotting flesh in my nostrils today.

The Company Commander had me play retreat every evening from the highest point overlooking the harbour, just to remind everyone who was boss, so I played 'The Nut Brown Maiden', the Company March, and 'Heilan' Laddie'. From where I played you could see in the shallow water thousands and thousands of craters from the bombing which made it look like the surface of the moon. Elsewhere the destruction was fantastic. Huge guns flung from their mountings, the houses just heaps of rubble and everything covered with a thick film of red dust.

Afterwards we spent a few days with the Third Battalion (part of the Guards Armoured Division) in Schleswig Holstein and I got to hear about Captain Runcie's escapade. Apparently just after the surrender he and a friend went for a row in a dinghy just offshore in the Baltic. Suddenly a few yards away an enormous U Boat surfaced and they felt pretty small and naked. Captain Runcie (the future Archbishop of Canterbury) with great presence of mind drew his revolver and fired a couple of shots into the air, whereupon the entire crew came out with their hands up. He was officially credited with capturing an enemy submarine!

We were sent back to the battalion at Wipperfurth, near Cologne for a few days when I was sent with Left Flank to Potsdam to form the British Guard of Honour at the forthcoming conference between Churchill, Truman and Stalin. The Russians refused at first to let us cross the Elbe, but finally we crossed at Magdeburg. I remember seeing trainloads of German POWs heading east. I wonder what became of them. We were in a tented camp at Potsdam and must have done seven or eight guards of honour for all the visiting dignitaries. There were of course the other foreign contingents doing much the same. During the conference Churchill lost the General Election and Attlee replaced him. I shall always remember him coming straight up to me, a mere Lance Corporal and shaking my hand and thanking me for my playing. One day I recall we had two Scots Guards sentries on the gates to the Schloss Cecilienhof, where the conference was being held, when Stalin approached completely surrounded by 20-25 heavily armed soldiers. The sentries quite correctly presented arms and Stalin's body guard were so jumpy they cocked their weapons and I thought we were all going to get shot. My mouth was so dry I don't think I've ever played so badly.

I got on quite well with one particular Red Army soldier who played the balalaika, a Russian stringed instrument a bit like a guitar. We used to go down to the café near the station and give impromptu recital to the (mainly German) clientele. One day as we met up by the gate he unslung his machine pistol and pushed it into my chest. I thought I was for it. Apparently an order from on high had come through forbidding fraternization and I think he must have been being watched, because after a couple of days of us being confined to barracks it all blew over.

I remember two beautiful blonde German girls, sisters, who came to do our laundry and keep the place tidy. One of them was taken by the Russians and repeatedly raped. She committed suicide. We got to Berlin proper once or twice and were duly impressed by the destruction. We took our turn to guard Spandau prison where I recall seeing Rudolf Hess and I remember vividly when a British lorry with a consignment of bully beef crashed we were stuffing tins of bully into our pockets – and so was everybody else, including the Russians!

Eventually we got back to the battalion at Wipperfurth, but I remember at the time getting a real buzz of excitement at what was going on at Potsdam. We really were witnessing history being made.

Norman Mitchell
Grenadier Guards

Norman, a Londoner by birth was born at Holloway in 1920 and like so many of his generation left school at 15 to seek employment. This he found in the City with a firm of stockbrokers until 1940, when tired of waiting to be called up he enlisted in the Grenadier Guards.

Arriving at Chelsea Barracks amongst those he encountered was his squad instructor, a certain Ted Bolan who by coincidence is now in the same ward with Norman at the Royal Hospital and thus only a short step from where they first met over sixty years ago.

Field training took place at Windsor with a return to Wellington Barracks. At that time with Britain under threat of German invasion troops were deployed in a defensive role around London – but not quite the ring of steel we hear of to-day. Pill boxes hastily constructed were waterlogged, weapons rusted and at the Blackwall Tunnel Norman was posted to keep an eye out not only for seaplanes landing but also U boats surfacing in the Thames. Slightly more dangerous one morning after the all clear had been sounded at Hungerford Bridge was the discovery of a landmine swinging precariously from its parachute caught on the bridge girders. The R.E. who defused it in fact won the George Cross.

The excitement of Home Service ended with the formation of the 6th Bn in October 1941 and embarkation for the Middle East in 1942 followed by a hectic 2,000 mile dash to join the 8th Army at the Medenine for an attack on the Mareth Line of which his story tells. Italy then beckoned via Salerno and a stopover for the Battle of Camino where of all things Norman, now a Platoon Sergeant suffered from an attack of frostbite which is still a painful reminder.

In 1945 he returned to the UK ready to tackle the Japanese, but was spared that confrontation by the events of Hiroshima and Nagasaki and the end of hostilities. So it was back to the Middle East and Palestine as an Orderly Room Sergeant, where a posting to Cairo found him at Central Records and a meeting with his future wife then in the ATS. She returned home to be joined by

Norman in marriage and the pending hope of release but it was not to be.

Wellington Barracks appeared on the scene yet again where from 1950-55 he had the great fortune not only to take over the Regimental Record Office but also on the eve of the Coronation in 1953 was promoted to ORQMS with the added responsibility of wearing a sword!

With this rank he moved to Dusseldorf, but such are the vagaries of service life that two years later he found himself at Lossiemouth with the Fleet Air Arm as a Ground Liaison Officer, a non-flying duty which he fulfilled until his discharge in 1958 after 18 years service.

Speed of a different sort in civilian life came with work in the Research Laboratory of Vanwall Racing Cars founded by Tony Vandervell, followed by employment until retirement in 1980 as Buyer for the Research Division of Rio Tinto. Norman was sadly widowed a year after he moved to Gloucester, but later remarried in 1984 a former colleague from Rio Tinto with whom he shared the next twenty years until her death in 2004, after which he decided to don the scarlet again at Chelsea, but this time across the road at the Royal Hospital.

Some Patrol!

Norman Mitchell

In March 16th 2005 whilst sitting in the comfortable surroundings of my conservatory and enjoying both my garden and the sunshine, my mind wandered back to another March 16th sixty two years ago in 1943. This time the sun of Tunisia played upon a different landscape far from the placid scene I now enjoyed.

Two weeks earlier the 2nd Scots Guards and 3rd Coldstreams had taken on Rommel's Panzers in a bloody encounter at Medenine whilst we of the 6th Bn Grenadiers had been held in reserve in order to take part in an attack to test the Mareth Line defences that lay ahead of us in the desert.

We were well trained, fit and superbly led and even Monty had honoured us with a visit and in his clipped tones had assured us that 'when I give a party it will be a good party and this will be a good party.'

Divisional Intelligence had passed on the information to us that the position was only lightly held with few mines laid so it would in fact be as the Field Marshal said 'a good party'.

So we prepared. 'Stand To' came and went so did breakfast and the rest of the day interspersed with a great deal of strong dark tea drunk from chipped enamel mugs – unlike the coffee I now enjoyed at home.

Weapons were cleaned again and again, magazines loaded, unloaded, reloaded to make sure they were in good order. Vehicles had last minute checks, engines run and rerun whilst Colonel Archer and his officers moved amongst us and chatted. We were all superbly confident, ready to go – it was just another day.

However, far from the truth was the battle that took place, certainly not a good party in any respect. Heavy fighting ensued and the 'few mines' we discovered to be two enormous minefields and on arrival we found ourselves facing crack German 90th Light Division troops plus the might of the 15th Panzers who naturally took their toll with the result that total casualties involved were 23 officers and 256 other ranks during the course of the attack.

Somewhat ironically at home the BBC announced on the 17th March

'Last night there was heavy patrol activity at a position near the Tunisian border'.

Some patrol! And it makes one wonder whether the term military intelligence is not something of a misnomer.

The memory of that night is often brought to mind, especially by letters and contact with those remaining of our small group and what a comparison between these two days over half a century apart.

Donald Pickering
The Royal Signals

Born at Wolverhampton in 1920 the youngest of a family of three brothers and three sisters such was the burden of family life at that time that at 14 he left school on a Friday and was at work the following Monday as a Parcel Boy with Midland Red Buses. This was followed with a spell until 16 with Manders the paint manufacturers finishing up at Boulton & Paul building aircraft such as the now forgotten two seater Hawker Demon biplane.

By then war clouds were gathering and the staff were informed that they would be in a reserved occupation on the outbreak of hostilities. Donald, however, decided differently and took the next day off and joined the Royal Signals on an 8 years in the Colours 4 on the Reserve.

Training as a Wireless Operator Signals followed in the chilly wastes of Catterick and the prospect of a draft to China with his kit bag marked. However, Hitler decided differently and instead he went to the Middle East via the tourist route across France by rail to Marseilles boarding HMTS Devonshire to Haifa and thence to Jerusalem with sorties in and out of Egypt, Palestine and Iraq, but luckily keeping clear of serious conflict.

Returning to GHQ Cairo his reputation had obviously preceded him with his skill at morse and he was selected to join SOE as an operator. With them he worked both in Italy and the UK until 1945 during which time he had tapped into the interest of Betty his future wife also working as an operator with the FANYs. With the end of the war he was unceremoniously sent back to his unit and his wife to be was demobbed and he later joined 1st Corps Signals in Belgium to train RASC drivers as operators on Landing Craft – quite a pointless exercise he thought until he discovered that it was in preparation for the invasion of Japan. From this he was saved by the dropping of the Atom bombs. Post war Germany was the next posting and from Dortmund he came home to marry Betty in September 1945 with whom he spent 56 happy years during which they produced a son and daughter.

As his period of service ran out the offer of an immediate commission tempted him until he spotted at the last minute in the small type that if he had signed he would have to serve a minimum of two years. Betty was not keen on the idea so he declined the kind offer remembering what happened to him the last time he signed up.

With his wide experience in signals he soon found employment in the field of communications with Standard and Telephone Cables with involvement in private systems for Scotland Yard and the American Embassy etc. ending up as Customer Services Manager.

1968 signalled his desire to go it alone and the idea of a village store beckoned. However, Betty fancied the licensed trade so mine hosts Donald and Betty took over the Ship Hotel at Bala in Merioneth for the next 16 years during which he became involved with the Licensed Victuallers Association and became Chairman of the Welsh Region.

Time was called in 1984 at the age of 64 with retreat to a cottage at Gwynedd and following the death of his wife and sadly both his daughter and son-in-law in 2006, he decided to enjoy the hospitality of the bar at the Royal Hospital but this time from the other side of the counter.

Get Me to the Church on Time
Donald Pickering

In 1944 with expiry of my five years abroad and being 'Python Protected' I said 'arrividerci' to the sunshine of Italy and with lips still sealed as a member of SOE I returned to the U.K. Not a very auspicious return, for whilst on my first leave in five years and wearing my brother's suit, I was berated and accused of cowardice by a woman passenger on a bus whose son, unlike me, was fighting for his country. Not too politely I asked her where she thought my tan had come from and demanded that the bus stop and let me off – one shouldn't jump to conclusions!

Henley on Thames was my next posting and there signals of mutual attraction were passed between myself and my future wife Betty who was in the FANYs training to be an operator with SOE. From there I was sent to Grendon Underwood in Buckinghamshire. Known as Station 53a, it had Nissen huts in its grounds and was home to 400 signallers and coders, mostly members of the FANY. My job was to train these operators who were essential to SOE and received special training in codes, ciphers and security checks and what made this work even more interesting was that they all came from different walks of life and a great social mix.

Once trained, as Betty became, it was on to the transmitting station at Poundon Hall not far from Grendon. Here we were in constant touch with the many agents throughout Europe with code names related to flowers and birds. In one case Betty actually had a contact serving in the German Army transmitting as they did from their amazing suitcase sets.

An SAS friend of mine was at that time working out of Germany and as it happened transmitting to Betty. On one occasion she had difficulty taking down his somewhat erratic morse and therefore sent him the official admonition 'Please improve signal'. Some weeks later he walked into the office demanding to know who had rebuked him. I didn't give the game away and he said 'How could I improve my signal when I was virtually up to my neck in water and being shot at by the Germans'! All's well that ends well and he later became godfather to our son George and daughter Carol.

One of my most nail biting experiences, however, did not involve the heat of battle or undercover activities. It was in fact my attempts to get married to Betty who was waiting in the U.K. In 1945 whilst stationed in Dortmund I was given leave to tie the knot and set off with hopes set high. These were dashed on Thursday when on arrival at Calais I found all leave boats cancelled due to rough weather. This continued over Friday and my deadline at the altar was 16.00 hours on the Saturday. No mobiles or emails in those days as time ticked away. Dawn on the Saturday morning saw me at the RTO's office, almost echoing the famous song 'Get me to the church on time' and despite the build up of numbers I managed to get a place on the boat. On arrival at Portsmouth there was a dramatic dash for a train and equally frantic rush across London, finally arriving home at 14.15 hours and just about enough time to spruce up and be ready to greet my bride at the altar at 16.00 hours!!

How many of the hundreds of signals we sent and received played an important part in the outcome of war we shall never know but I am proud to have been chosen to play a small part in it and hoped that in every case as the motto of the Signals says that they were 'swift and sure'.

Bill Cross
Royal Scots Greys
The Life Guards

The army was obviously in Bill's blood from birth for his father had served with the Coldstream Guards in the Great War and like so many who did return home was scarred by his experiences and made even worse by the death of his wife in 1917 giving birth to Bill. Her place was later taken by a wonderful stepmother and two stepbrothers and sisters, a large family to bring up in those difficult times especially with the death of his father at 37. Thus it was with some sorrow that he was collected by his maternal grandmother and taken away to live at Wokingham, a short and troubled relationship ending with his placement in an orphanage and later in the Gordon Boys Home at Brookwood where his five-year military and musical career began.

In 1934 at 17 he enlisted as a Band Boy (trumpeter) in the Cavalry of the Line the Royal Scots Greys and after training at

Edinburgh and London he found himself as a mounted musician playing at such events as the Jubilee of George V in 1935 and later the Coronation of George VI in 1936.

But pageantry was replaced by Palestine in 1938, still with horses which were later replaced by motorised lorries from Glubb Pasha's Arab Legion and later by Sherman tanks. Following the outbreak of war in 1941 they moved into Syria and amongst other things with the fall of France and the establishment of the Vichy regime found themselves confronting the Foreign Legion by whom they were captured, marched to Damascus and held prisoner for six weeks. The destruction of the French fleet at Mers el Kebir reversed the roles with the French surrendering but the chagrin at one time of being in a Guard of Honour for a senior Vichy figure still rankles.

It was back to the regiment and into the desert and serious action with Shermans that followed at Sidi Burrani facing Rommel's Panzers being pushed back. During a lull and a brew up for tea they were attacked by shells and Bill unable to reach the safety of his tank was wounded and came-to blinded in both eyes and on board an aircraft heading for a military hospital run by the South Africans on Canal zone.

Following treatment he regained enough sight in one eye for him not only to see but also get involved at El Alamein and Tripoli. Later on with vehicles waterproofed the unit landed at Salerno in support of 56 Black Cat Division and thence on through Italy via such hot spots as Monte Cassino and the typhus ridden city of Naples at that time, all of which he survived.

D Day loomed ahead and so it was home to the UK to prepare for Operation Overlord as part of the 22nd Armoured Brigade again equipped with Shermans. The reception on Sword Beach did not go as planned. However, survive he did and with the Allied armies advanced through the Low Countries to Wismar and the Baltic Coast where the war finished.

In 1945 scarlet and plumes appeared again and for the next 19 years as a member of the Life Guards he participated in virtually every Royal and State occasion not only opening of Parliament, State Visits but also the Coronation of Queen Elizabeth II, collecting not only her Coronation Medal but also the Jubilee Medal, not including his two foreign awards from Nepal and Persia for Royal duties during a State visit.

Music didn't stop with retirement in 1964 for he then donned the uniform of the HAC Band with whom he played for the next 14 years thus adding yet another ribbon to the row. Time was also found to play music outside the military sphere with bands and in clubs. Whilst his civilian employment was as varied as his military career, at one time a bouncer in the Casualty Department of Minehead Hospital, where size counted, and later at the Law Courts in the Strand and Barclays Bank.

It was in 2002 that he returned to a military life by joining the Royal Hospital Chelsea, where, of course, music is still very much a part of life as he plays in the Royal Hospital Band.

Alf Hey
The Royal Artillery

Not only the son of a soldier, (his father served with the Northumberland Fusiliers in WWI), but also the father of a soldier who served with the Prince of Wales Regiment. Alf was born at Gomersal, Yorkshire in 1921. Schooldays over at 14, he became a Garden Boy at a private house for the princely sum of 14s. (70p) a week, a wage he drew until he was old enough to enlist on May 8th 1939 at Cleckheaton into the Duke of Wellington's Regiment. He was then rebadged into the Royal Artillery to serve with 234 Bty 89 Heavy Ack Ack Regiment in Kent but not for long, for he was soon aboard the troopship 'Canterbury' kitted out for Egypt.

January 1941 saw him afloat again on the 'Ulster Prince' bound for Crete, where after hiding in the hills overnight, the guns were dug in during the next day ready for action.

Plenty of this followed and they were in constant action as air defence of Suda Bay until overrun during the invasion of May

1941, Alf being one of seven survivors out of a Battery of 54, the casualties being inflicted by German paratroops. During this struggle Alf was wounded in both legs by shrapnel. Help came in the form of the Royal Marines who rescued him and put him in a temporary sick bay in a local school. However, this freedom was short lived as the Germans overran the position and in July was taken prisoner. After being confined in a local prison for a month with work including shifting stones with mules to build a war memorial, it was back to sea again, this time to Greece and the notorious camp at Salonika.

The next stage included a somewhat crowded train journey sharing a cattle truck with 72 other passengers for seven days with only half a loaf of bread and no facilities. The destination was a transit camp at Lamsdorf near Leipzig already holding about 30,000 prisoners. Working parties offered some form of relief and three month stretches were spent employed in forestry, railways or underground in salt or coal mines.

Gunfire heralded the approach of the Russians in 1945 so it was time to be on the move again and several thousand inmates set off in freezing cold and six feet or more of snow on a 1,000 mile march, not only losing casualties from hunger and exhaustion, but worst of all being strafed by our own side. In addition to the loss of prisoners, the German guards also defected, and of the original 97 that set out, only 7 remained when they finally arrived at Steinbeck where they were rescued by the advancing Americans in April 1945.

Repatriation via Rheims, Guildford and Morpeth took place and he was finally discharged on October 24th 1945 after 6 years and 5 months service.

Post-war Britain produced a wide variety of employment ranging from window cleaner, gardener and finally store-man/ driver where he enjoyed the freedom of being his own boss and no longer taking orders. Retiring at 74 with memories of Crete's blue skies and scenery, he moved there, and in happier circumstances with his son and family who opened a snack bar and enjoyed life to the full. However, the past was not forgotten, and indeed is still remembered and even to-day, though now at Chelsea, he regularly attends the ceremonies at memorials around the island, together with ex partisan comrades who welcome the scarlet with pride.

HOWZAT?
Crete, Cricket and a Very Long Walk
Alf Hey

One has heard of love at first sight and that is how I felt when I saw Crete in 1941 with its beautiful scenery and skies. However, the relationship was somewhat spoilt with the arrival of the Germans, not as we now joke about as tourists, but as paratroopers. We had dug in as air defence for Suda Bay to protect the shipping from air attack by Stukas and Heinkels by firing over open sights; indeed such was the terrain that the guns in the hills were actually firing *down* on the bombers as they flew in.

With the inevitable fall of Greece news reached us that we were the next to be invaded and the increased bombing proved so. We took to our trenches and eventually saw German paratroops advancing through the olive groves, machine gunning and hurling grenades as they came. It was sheer murder and we were virtually defenceless. One of the grenades not only blew my boots off but wounded me in both legs and I lay immobilised awaiting my fate. However, the Royal Marines rescued us and took me to a temporary hospital in a local school. But freedom was short lived for it was overrun by the enemy and I was 'in the bag' as a POW.

Imprisonment followed for a while in the local nick, during which time we were forced to build a German war memorial with stones carried by mules. We then said farewell, in my case au revoir, to Crete and embarked for a 2-3 day journey to Greece. The infamous 'Hell Camp' at Salonika awaited us – appalling conditions, beri-beri was rife, as I painfully discovered, whilst the trigger happy guards weren't averse to shooting those they took a dislike to. After a seemingly endless month, we were marched to the railway station and packed into cattle trucks – 70-80 in each, standing room only. Rations for what was to be a seven day journey was half a loaf and with only two 'comfort stops' en route and, to put it crudely, and in reality, we 'shat where we sat'.

Our destination proved to be Lamsdorf Camp near Leipzig – here the guards were more tolerant and amenable having come from the Russian front, so knew about suffering. That could not be said of the fleas that inhabited my single issue blanket. With a population of 30,000 inmates, Lamsdorf wasn't quite Butlins, but some form of respite could be obtained by volunteering for outside work. At various times I was employed in three month stints in forestry, railways, and not so pleasantly in coal and salt mines. In the latter we wore paper suits and clogs and the effect of the salt on our skins wasn't too good.

Harking back to Butlins, there were some moments when humour helped save the day. We had contact with other camps and each week it was decided that a particular day would be nominated 'Silly Day' with a chosen theme. Thus one week it was cricket, so to the Germans complete mystification, two cricket teams assembled, no equipment, but mimed the whole ritual of the game, overs, scores, etc. At one point a batsman was struck in the eye by a ball so medics rushed out, bandaged him and led him, not only off the pitch, but to the gate. Here a sentry enquired what was wrong and was told of the 'injury' and that he needed to go to the sick bay whereupon he opened the gates and let them out!

On another occasion we used to make a brew, hardly alcohol but made of anything we could find, potato peelings, raisins, herbs, etc. The Germans got wind of our 'brewing' and tried to put a stop to it, so one day we prepared the ingredients but added a little extra in the form of generous contributions of urine. The potion was set on the stove, stirred vigorously, the door burst open and our triumphant captors not only seized the illicit brew, but to our delight took it away and drank some of it!

Potatoes also served in another ruse. We used to work in a canning factory where we peeled thousands of potatoes to be tinned for the German army. This we did, adding to the contents large numbers of pebbles and stones that we hoped would have cracking results on their dentistry.

As the war progressed, and we did have secret radios, we heard of the Russians' advance, and so in the bleakest of winter with snow 6-8 feet high, it was decided to move us further West – in fact 1,000 miles further, a distance we did at the rate of 30 miles a day. Conditions were terrible; not only did we lose men from hunger and exhaustion, but also from 'friendly fire' as our planes, seeing such a mass of men assumed we were German pioneers en route to repair bridges. Eventually this was stopped by setting ourselves out in the form of the letters 'P.O.W.' and how relieved we were when the planes did a victory roll to let us know they understood.

Food en route was virtually non existent. We ate anything and everything. I could discuss the merits of cat against dog or raw sugar beet against mangels and other delicacies. In fact I cannot bear to see food wasted even now, and for some time after my return at the end of a meal my family would spot me putting the odd half unfinished slice of bread into my pocket – old habits died hard.

Finally we fetched up in Steinbeck, with only 7 of the original 97 guards remaining. The rest had defected en route. Here we were packed into a large barn and kept a low profile as the SS were in the village. One day, climbing into a pigeon loft (food again) we spotted an American GI armed to the teeth and smoking a cigar. We signalled to him, and before long the American tanks rolled in and cleared the village and we were at last freed.

Repatriation took place via Rheims where I lost my travelling companions of lice and fleas. We were fed (not too much) and well looked after – then home via Guildford and Morpeth, where amazingly my mental health and sanity was checked by a very complicated scientific test 'assembling a torch'. This mastered, I was declared free to go and was discharged on October 24th 1945.

Despite everything, the memories of Crete remained, and so after some time in various employments I achieved my dream and in 1984 moved to an apartment in Crete joined by my son and his family. I lived there for a wonderful five and a half years, and even now still return surrounded by so many memories and the incredible friendship of the people amongst whom I lived and fought.

Douglas Huxley MBE MM
The Grenadier Guards

The effect of the Great War in addition to the vast toll of lives also had repercussions upon those who came after. Particularly so in the case of Douglas Huxley who was born in 1920 at Preston. The son of a Royal Artillery man who returned from France unable to face life and its responsibilities the family of four children as in many cases was maintained by his mother whose skill as a weaver at the Horrockses mill kept them until 1924. Then with the downturn of the cotton industry unemployment was rife and so Douglas found himself in the local workhouse where his mother, as a laundress, kept them fed and clothed. It was the stigma of the latter that affected the young boy and so at 14 he ran away and managing to avoid the searching police worked as a farm labourer which not only helped build his character and strength but at the age of 16 helped him to convince the Grenadier Guards to accept him.

However, truth will out and eventually his age was rumbled, but rather than lose a willing recruit he was in 1937 sent to the 3rd Bn at Windsor as a Drummer Boy for the pay of 11s. (55p) a day until he reached maturity at 18 when he signed on for nine years with the Colours and three with the Reserve.

At Windsor his experience with horses on the farm stood him in good stead and he made quite a name for himself. The late thirties heard the rumblings of war in both Czechoslovakia and later in Poland when the troops were mobilised at Aldershot. Preliminary training for mechanical warfare consisted of an Austin with dual control which was driven night and day by those being prepared for tank warfare.

1938 sadly saw the horses despatched to Melton Mowbray for slaughter and the rumour that they were made into pies and in their place vehicles began to arrive for serious war manoeuvres at Aldershot. War was declared in 1939 but as Douglas was still under age for combat he returned to Windsor for duty with the boy solders and those unfit to fight. Thus he missed action with the BEF and the nightmare of Dunkirk.

Now an Instructor Lance Sgt. and old enough and wanting to join the scrap he joined the 4th Bn Guards Armoured Division and set off to war. Training in tank tactics, gunnery and wireless followed and having passed out as a full Sgt. was accepted into Squadron No. 3 under a superb and unforgettable Squadron Leader, Ivor Crosthwaite. At this point with the future so uncertain Douglas and his fiancée Betty whom he had known since she was 15 decided to do something positive and so in 1943 married and despite the interruption of war managed to enjoy not only nearly sixty years together but also generate 29 grandchildren from the union.

Promoted to Troop Leader with three Churchill tanks for which training was given and later put into practice on D Day with a landing at Gold Beach and a follow on through Europe to the Rhine. At Munster his actions were rewarded with the MM and at Lubeck he became engaged in naval warfare shelling a U-Boat in the Kiel Canal.

Such were the Infantry casualties at that time that he was withdrawn from tanks and became a member of the PBI eventually returning to the UK to prepare for the invasion of Japan, only to be saved like so many others by the dropping of the atomic bomb. Khaki Drill and Palestine followed until 1948 thence to Tripoli but with the arrival of Colonel Nasser and a certain lack of hospitality it was home again this time as a Drill Sgt.

Health in the form of an ulcer intervened and so it was somewhat lighter duties at Mons Officer Cadet School under the legendary RSM Brittain where he was made CSM to the Royal Artillery officer cadets. Fitness returned but sadly no post back with the regiment so again he was given an instructional role at Arborfield Apprentices School but his heart was in London and eventual pleas were answered when he finished his 25 years of service in 1961 as CSM to the London University OTC.

But uniformed life wasn't over thanks to a good military connection of which you will read, he became Assistant Doorkeeper at the House of Lords rising to Principal holder of the post and during his twenty five years served five Black Rods and followed the official job description of 'Policing the Chamber of the House of Lords and looking after the comfort of their Lordships'.

Comfort of another sort this time. His own began in 2003 when he moved to the

Royal Hospital and was delighted one day to spot through a window a fellow Grenadier Harry Webb whom he had met in 1937 but now in the Welsh Guards.

Soft Soap & Silk Finish
Douglas Huxley

Memories very much resemble an album of old photographs which are thumbed through from time to time picking out events and people, some rather faded in black and white and others much brighter in colour.

So I have decided rather than tell one long story of 'derring do' I would offer a few snapshots from my life. The soap story is not in any way related to a TV series but covers an incident in my very early days at Windsor when with a looming kit inspection I was minus my bar of soap, either flogged or stolen. With minutes to spare I rushed to the cookhouse and persuaded a mate to cut me a square of cheese which looked and probably tasted like soap! Standing by my bed I was horrified to see that the officer carrying out the inspection was accompanied not only by the CSM but also his dog. Needless to say the latter soon detected the difference between soap and cheese and was up on the bed scattering the layout and made off with the loot. His owner grabbed him and was about to punish him when I spoke up and admitted my deceit not wishing to see the dog taking the blame. Next day on a charge and appearing before the said officer and awaiting punishment I was in fact let off due, I think, because we both had a fellow feeling for animals.

In my career notes there is a mention of my Squadron Leader, Major Ivor Crosthwaite MC and he I think would need a book of his own, a great officer and friend with whom we shared many experiences. It was Major Crosthwaite I think who invented what we now call aromatherapy. Prior to an action or at any time when we were tensed up we would go to him and what might be misconstrued today 'ask for a sniff'. He would then produce from his pocket a bottle of the most exquisite perfume a whiff of which worked like magic on our senses and settled our nerves wonderfully, I only wish I knew its name. Another time in Germany he liberated some bows and arrows from an archery school and the following day going into action he appeared out of his turret firing arrows at the Germans. Searching the wood later he was somewhat disappointed to find no casualties as he hoped the enemy would have been mystified by the use of such weaponry. Speaking of turrets, I would never go into action with the lid open and kept it firmly closed. My first day in action I saw officers needlessly killed by not closing down and exposing themselves to enemy fire.

One of the most wonderful sights I have ever seen and which could never be recreated in any block buster film was the first sight of the Rhine with literally thousands of aircraft in the sky and troops moving forward over boat bridges. It was at that moment I knew we had won the war though shortly afterwards near Munster I nearly ended my part in it when I was allowed to move forward to attack a position and my tank was hit and I had to bale out – not the best of situations. News reached us at that time of an unusual engagement by one of our squadron one could almost call it a naval engagement for at Lubeck as they approached the Kiel Canal they found a very large tin fish in the shape of a U Boat which they engaged – I don't know who was most surprised!

During my service I came across many people of varied rank and position one of them being Major General Sir Brian Horrocks under whom I served as a Troop Leader. During a break in the fighting he once discussed life after the war and said I should look him up if ever I needed work – little did he know!

In 1960 I went to watch the State Opening of Parliament and there amongst the dignitaries gathered and indeed a principal player I spotted Sir Brian resplendent as Black Rod. Nothing ventured nothing gained. I managed to gatecrash his cocktail party at the House of Lords and on meeting him reminded him of his promise. True to his word the next day I went for an interview and was eventually appointed Assistant Doorkeeper to the House of Lords and later Principal Doorkeeper, posts I held for 25 years.

During this time I witnessed a great deal of history and at times hilarity from the traditional search each November by the Yeoman of the Guard to the keeping of peace within the House.

On one occasion I was informed that trouble had broken out in the Peeresses Gallery and on investigation I discovered that it was being caused by none other than the actress Vivien Leigh together with some very voluble friends protesting about the closure of I think the St. James Theatre. I informed Sir Brian who the culprits were and his orders were 'Go and invite them to tea'. I duly explained that Sir Brian was very displeased but would like them to join him for tea. 'Delighted' purred Lady Olivier and off they trooped – problem solved. I don't think this sort of treatment would work in to-day's climate.

There are many more tales I could tell of those years but I think they would need a whole book and a little discretion but hopefully you will have enjoyed these few snaps from the album.

Charlie Dale
The Irish Guards

Charlie is a Londoner, born in Islington in 1924. He was one of 13 children 'which made life a bit hard' and not all his siblings survived to adulthood. His father was a master plumber and was not always in work.

Charlie's schooling was severely interrupted by an accident in which his leg was run over by a horse and cart during a Pearly Kings' procession, a popular event in those days. He left school at 14 and had various odd jobs. His father, clearly one of the old school, threw the boys out of the house at 16 to find their own way in the world. He joined the Air Training Corps at the outbreak of war and volunteered for the Royal Air Force, but failed the selection. He was called up in 1942, decided to join the Guards and was put down for the Irish Guards without any further ceremony. He did his 15 week recruit training at the Guards Depot at Caterham and was then sent to the Irish Guards Training Battalion at Lingfield, where they successfully mucked up the racecourse! He did some King's Guards in 1943 after which the battalion was sent to Scotland, first to Hawick and then to Edinburgh.

Charlie was a dab hand at the 3 inch mortar and was in the 2nd Battalion Irish Guards when they landed in Normandy in July 1944 as part of the Guards Armoured Division. Unfortunately his mortaring skills were not so much in demand and he became a plain infantryman. The battalion made its way towards Paris but was stopped short of the French capital for the French and Americans to take the city. They pushed forward very fast towards Belgium mounted on tanks, met up with the Americans short of Brussels and crossed the Escaut Canal on Joe's Bridge (Lieutenant Colonel JOE Vandeleur was commanding officer.)

The Guards Armoured Division was advancing in support of the Arnhem landings but the going was restricted to only one road and a few tracks. During an engagement at this time Charlie was very severely wounded in the leg and hand by machine gun fire and evacuated from the combat zone and back to England where he spent the next year in hospital and convalescing.

Charlie was medically discharged on

account of his wounds and in spite of a badly deformed hand started work as a television inspector where, as he smilingly remembers, he was able to watch the 1948 Olympics as part of his job. Thereafter he remained an electrical and mechanical TV inspector until his retirement in 1989.

Charlie married in 1952 and his daughter was born two years later. Sadly his wife died of cancer in 1982 and Charlie remarried in 1986 having moved to Ashford. His second wife also died of cancer in 1996 and, having heard of the Royal Hospital Chelsea through his contacts in the Royal British Legion, he joined the Scarlet ranks in November 2005. Charlie works as an Assistant Librarian and is sometimes to be seen cutting about in a smart red electric buggy, though, as he says, he still likes to use his legs while he can, though the hundred yard dash does take a minute or two.

A Real Hole in My Wallet
Charlie Dale

It was September 1944. We had just liberated Brussels and had been on the receiving end of a joyful welcome from the inhabitants.

There was cheering and waving of flags and tears of happiness but all of a sudden we were told to get moving again. It wasn't till we reached the Escaut Canal to secure the bridges that we understood the reason for the haste. The Guards Armoured Division, of which we were a part were (among others) racing to support the parachute landings at Arnhem. We infantry were being carried on Sherman tanks of the battalion and sped northwards until we reached the Dutch border when the order came to halt for the night and dig in. We got our heads down and next morning thankfully the supply chain caught up with us and we had a good breakfast. It must have been the 16th September.

We were ordered to advance on foot straight after breakfast and soon came under heavy and sustained machine gun and mortar fire which seemed to be coming from some open ground in front of us. The company dived into some woods to work our way forward under cover. The tanks, of course, could not advance through the woods. We had evidently been seen entering the woods as enemy fire still rained down onto us. My platoon sergeant was hit in the face and at the same time I felt a small tug at my arm and was surprised to see blood running down it. The bullet had gone clean through. I carried on and saw a German soldier with a box of ammunition running across my front. I fired at him from the range of about 50 yards and he disappeared, but I don't know if I hit him or not. I then took cover behind a small tree. There was a hell of a lot of noise – we were in contact and both sides were firing, mostly small arms with the occasional crack of a mortar bomb exploding – as well as the shouting of orders and the screams of those who had been hit.

It was in this heat of battle that I forgot one of the cardinal rules of fieldcraft. When you take cover you immediately move your position – you never, ever get up from the position where you disappeared. I rose from cover and that was the last I knew. I came round (I suppose) a minute or so later in time to hear the shouted order to withdraw. I was lying on my back, having been spun round by the impact of the bullets. I moved my left leg, but my foot wouldn't move and my left hand had also been hit. I remember clearly even after all these years thinking 'I wish I had a Bren. I could go on to firing with my other hand.'

Although I must have been in shock and was only semi-conscious I saw I was lying in a small dry ditch. It may be that I had instinctively dragged myself into cover – I don't know. I do recall seeing one of our own tanks rumbling towards me one track in my ditch! Fortunately it stopped a few yards short of me and then reversed. Maybe someone saw me because some time later (I have no idea how long but I do recall noting that the sun had moved) I was picked up by some medics in a Bren gun carrier. I drifted in and out of consciousness as they took me back to the forward aid post where I recall looking at the blood bag attached to my body and being surprised at how quickly it seemed to empty. I was told later that I had lost as much blood as I could have. I was asked whether I wanted a cigarette but I refused in favour of some water; I was told it was sweet tea or nothing!

At the Field Hospital they removed 15 pieces of bone from my leg plus a piece of cellophane from my wallet which I had been carrying in my map pocket. Some French banknotes had holes in them and rather to my surprised they were exchanged without any problem. I had been hit by 4 Spandau bullets in the leg and some more in my left hand. It took bloody ages to be able to use a knife and fork again!

Carl Borley BME
Queens Royal Irish Hussars

Carl Borley cheerfully admits to be a 'barrack room rat', the son of a Corporal in the 5th Inniskilling Dragoon Guards who had fought in the First World War. Appropriately enough he was born in Aldershot in 1931 and the family quarter in Chetwoode Terrace still stands. Carl was the youngest of three sons and on his father's retirement the family moved up to Birmingham, his mother's home, where his father got a job with BSA.

Carl left school at 15 and joined his father's regiment as a Boy, initially joining the band as a tuba player, which he hated. He was sent to the Army School of Music at Kneller Hall but rebelled against this and went absent. This and the fact that he also flatly refused to play the tuba was not looked on kindly by the authorities, but eventually he got his wish and joined a troop of newly-issued Centurion tanks in Munster in 1949.

In the youthful hope and expectation of glory he transferred to the 8th Hussars who were being sent to Korea. The Regiment spent two active years there, followed by postings to Tidworth and Luneburg. In 1958 the Regiment amalgamated with the 4th Hussars to form the Queen's Royal Irish Hussars and moved to Hohne.

In 1960 Carl was posted to the Fighting Vehicles Research & Development Establishment at Chertsey as NCO in charge of floatation trials on a variety of armoured vehicles. He stayed there 3 years taking part in the schnorkelling trials with the newly-produced Chieftain tank, and was awarded the BEM. A return to the Regiment in Malaya followed, equipped with Saladin armoured cars and Ferret scout cars. This coincided with the attempts by the Indonesians to take over Brunei and Sarawak and the subsequent operations by the British Army to prevent these incursions. This involved both road patrols and foot patrols in the jungle. By this time Carl was a troop sergeant. A posting (as SQMS) to Wolfenbuttel followed after which the Regiment was sent to Bovington as RAC Centre Regiment and Carl was promoted to Squadron Sergeant Major. Learning that the next posting was to be Germany again, he managed to wangle a posting to Kuwait as a Gunnery and Tactical Armoured instructor where he remained for the final three years of his Army service, leaving in 1972.

For ten years Carl worked as a civilian Landrover driver at Bovington after which he worked in a double glazing company in Wareham, from which he retired in 1996 at the age of 65. Sadly his wife had died several years previously and after a few years of living on his own he decided the Scarlet coat of the Chelsea Pensioners was for him. Carl joined the Royal Hospital in May 2006 and is to be seen regularly helping to organise things in the Prince of Wales Hall, the Royal Hospital's social centre.

A Full Day's Work on the Imjin
Carl Borley

We landed at Pusan in Korea in the Autumn of 1950 as part of the United Nations contingent, and the first armoured regiment to be deployed there. The regiment was pretty quickly split up, the squadrons being attached to different brigades. I was the driver of a Mark 3 Centurion tank having been trained in England in my previous regiment, the Inniskillings.

Our brigade, the 29th Infantry Brigade, consisted of the Glosters, the Ulster Rifles and the Northumberland Fusiliers. We were ordered to take over from B Squadron and immediately moved forward and did a 30 mile recce – not a Chink in sight. We leaguered up for the night. It was the spring of 1951 and the nights were still pretty chilly. During the night the Chinese and North Koreans had moved into the area and we were stood to. Then they started an assault on the infantry positions along the Imjin River and we were sent up to support them, one troop per regiment. The situation was fairly confused as we moved up to the line and the enemy were clearly visible in masses on the opposite hillsides, even though we were closed down and my field of vision was limited to my driving periscope. There seemed to be a hell of a lot of them. (We later learned that each of our regiments was facing a North Korean Army!)

We started engaging them with the BESA machine gun, coaxially mounted with the main armament. Unfortunately, being such a precision weapon it was prone to an awful lot of faults and let us down badly. As we got closer we started to engage the enemy with our 17 pounder firing HE onto the hillsides at a range of a few hundred yards. This didn't seem to deter them one bit and soon we were amongst them, so much so that we were literally running them over as we advanced. Those that could clambered on board the tank in their efforts to get at us. We could see them yanking at the hatches and it took the combined efforts of all our tanks, firing machine guns (when they worked) at each other to dislodge them.

They were standing in front of us blazing away with their burp guns and laughing and blowing trumpets as if they thought they could stop a 50 ton tank. It was as if they were on drugs or something. We simply ran over them – they didn't half make a mess of the tracks. Looking back it doesn't seem real, but there was no time to be scared – I was too busy driving the tank and trying to avoid getting bogged down. I can tell you it was getting bloody hot in there, all closed down, the four of us sweating away at our jobs. And noisy, too. Aside from our own machine gun and main armament firing away we could clearly hear the sounds of our comrades' machine guns hosing down our turret trying to get the little so-and-so's off us.

Our object was still to get up to the infantry positions to support them and finally we made it. Things were still mighty confused, but there was a sort of lull and our chaps managed to get onto our tanks and lay the wounded on the engine covers. We were still supporting each other with direct fire when we could and must have made half a dozen trips forward and back collecting more casualties. The squadron lost five tanks in this engagement.

Finally we got the order to withdraw, short of petrol and ammo and not really able to do much more. The infantry positions had been overrun by this time.

Six weeks later we were sent back to recover our dead – not a pleasant job, particularly if you recognize them.

Bill Kent
The Royal Artillery

Bill is not, strictly speaking, a proper 'Brummie' having been born in Sutton Coldfield in 1913. His father was a baker and Bill, an only child, never knew his mother who died in the influenza pandemic of 1917. He was looked after by various members of his family including Grannie Kent who kept him on the straight and narrow until he left school in 1928 to seek employment.

Bill had joined the Royal Signals Volunteers in 1936 and lined the route of King George VI and Queen Elizabeth's Coronation in 1936. He then transferred to 45 Searchlight Battalion RE in Birmingham in 1938 and became the Colonel's driver. Early in 1942 they were transferred from searchlights to Bofors guns and became artillerymen. After training they were sent to India in 1943 and joined 525 Battery (8th Battalion The Gordon Highlanders) of 100 Ack Ack/Anti-Tank regiment. Bill took part in the battle of Kohima, using their Bofors anti-aircraft guns to defend the 25 pounder and 5.5 inch guns in the Zubza Box, a few miles from Kohima. After this about 40 gunners were transferred to the Infantry, and Bill quite literally swapped his Bofors gun for a Sten and a few grenades. The Cameron Highlanders were badly in need of battle casualty replacements, so that was where he ended up as a section commander. He served with the Camerons for the last year of the war and still reckons this period as one of the highlights of his life. He was re-transferred back to the Gordons in 1945.

After the war Bill became a traveller in fashion and then a fashion buyer in Birmingham and worked in a ladies dress firm until 1977. After that he worked for a glass company and for a gardening organisation still in Birmingham, finally retiring in 1983 at the age of 70.

Sadly his wife died in 2006 and not having any children he was left all alone in an anchor home near Berwick-upon-Tweed. The Royal Hospital was the obvious place to be and Bill joined the ranks in December 2006.

An Infantry Gunner in Burma - A Cameron Man
Bill Kent

If this title sounds a little strange – it was! After the battle of Kohima (June 1944) the Japanese were in full retreat. The airfields, airstrips and other defensive areas that had previously been defended by anti-aircraft personnel like me became redundant. The infantry had taken a lot of casualties in the battle and it made sense to transfer us across to make up the shortfall in 2 Div. Initially we were all a bit nervous as to how we would be received. It was not as if we were genuine Cameron Highlanders, trained by their own staff and well versed in the history of the Regiment. We needn't have worried. We were welcomed as badly needed replacements and swiftly made to feel at home.

After a busy settling in period we were given our orders. We were to clear the road from Imphal to Tamu, a distance of some 200 miles and re-supplied by air. How I longed for my 15 cwt towing my gun as we slogged into the foothills. They were the sort of hills that when you think you've reached the top you turn the corner and there is another one to be climbed. Lord, it was hot!

And the flies; they were a constant nuisance especially at mealtimes. You had one hand on your fork and the other constantly brushing them away. We took a daily mepacrine tablet against malaria, but when we came out of action they were no longer issued and many people, including me, went down with the disease.

Eventually we reached our objective, the village of Tamu. We didn't know whether there were any Japs still in it so we advanced very cautiously. The villagers, who were very much on our side, told us, unbelievably, 'don't worry, we told the Japs you were coming.' No amount of further questioning was of any use as they just laughed and walked away. Fully armed and extremely cautious, we entered the village. Everything was deathly quiet, no Jap sentries were in evidence, but we were expecting to be ambushed at any moment. We approached the first hut adopting the standard practice; one man with rifle held at the high port one side of the entrance which allowed his partner to duck quickly inside to cover the room. The first man followed immediately to give covering fire if necessary. What we saw was a depressing sight. Almost all the Japanese inside were dead, and the rest nearly so.

Every hut we searched was the same. They had been caught before they could cross the river and had died of starvation, disease and malnutrition. No wonder the villagers were laughing.

During the monsoon the weather was very changeable. We would tramp through the endless downpour with the red mud coming well over our boots, which would be followed in short order by beautiful hot, drying sun. I can recall once we stopped by a small waterfall and jumped in fully clothed. It washed away our sweat and also cleaned our clothes somewhat. Wonderfully refreshing! After reaching Tamu we were withdrawn to Milestone 82 north of Imphal and spent the next three months in comparative luxury readying ourselves for the big push into Burma.

Christmas 1944 saw us making a night crossing of the Chindwin at Kalewa over the then longest Bailey Bridge ever built and pressing on eastwards. It was much better marching by night for we could cover many more miles in the cool and could rest up during the heat of the day. We eventually arrived on to the wide open plain of Shwebo, a great loop of land enclosed by the Chindwin and Irrawaddy rivers, immediately north west of Mandalay. We had to push on as quickly as possible, clearing all the villages in our path. We knew when a village was 'clean' for the villagers came out to meet us. One village we came across made us immediately suspicious, for there was no sign of the population. We advanced with due caution and suddenly came under intense machine gun and small arms fire. We took cover and assessed the situation. Presently a Corporal, whom I didn't know, moved off in a flanking direction with two men. After only 20 yards they came under heavy machine gun fire and the Corporal was hit. All of a sudden there was a hush. Then Sergeant Harry White ordered mortar smoke to be directed at the area and, once the bombs had fallen, tore off his helmet and sprinted to the fallen man. He lifted him up and staggered back with him, lowered him back to the ground and said simply 'he's gone.' He then went back and brought the other two home. I have never seen such a heroic act.

We finally reached the Irrawaddy towards the end of January 1945. It had been a long slog on foot from the Chindwin. Now for the crossing. To start with our 15cwt trucks plied backwards and forwards on the home bank dragging bunches of brushwood behind them to raise a great cloud of dust and hopefully fool the Japs into thinking we were going to cross there. We did some practising with inflatable assault boats and on 24th February we were taken to our crossing point near Ngazun. At 2200 hours we pushed off, the spearhead of the 2 Div assault. It was a beautiful moonlit night as we paddled the 1500 yard width of the great river. Our objective was two white pagodas some 600 yards inland. Once there we were to send a patrol downstream to link up with the Worcesters. We were about half way across when we came under machine gun fire as the enemy saw our reflections in the water. Surprise was gone and the outboard motor was started up as we paddled like madmen for the far bank. Reaching it safely we scrambled ashore using the elephant grass to haul ourselves up the ten foot high bank and made for our objective. We failed to make contact with the Worcesters – we later learned that they had come under much heavier fire. We were a bit thin on the ground too having lost 13 Platoon altogether, but the bridgehead was finally secured and the rest of the Division was able to cross. And so the push began into south eastern Burma.

Not long afterwards the news came through that the Japs had all gone from our sector so we were able to be pulled out. I can remember very clearly that we were told to get rid of any excess weight, including arms and grenades, before embarking in the Dakotas for the flight back to India, so we dumped it all down the nearest well. I sometimes wonder what the locals must have thought when they found it!

I shall always be grateful that I was given the chance to fight alongside such terrific soldiers in the Cameron Highlanders and that I was paid the highest compliment of my life when they made me a 'Cameron Man'.

Arthur Masters
Argyll & Sutherland Highlanders

A Warwickshire lad by birth Arthur was born at Coventry in 1929. The son of a soldier who interestingly had not only added to his age to fight in the Great War but also reduced it to take part in WW II serving with the Scottish Rifles.

This Scottish connection continued for after a spell with an engineering firm on leaving school at 14, he enlisted at 17 in 1945, not as one would imagine in a local regiment, but in the Black Watch!

With them after training at Inverness he was posted out to India for the last days of the Raj as it happened seeing service in Karachi, Peshwar and a spell on the famous or infamous North West Frontier. With the disbanding of the 2nd Battalion in 1948 he donned the bonnet of the Argyll and Sutherland Highlanders at Fort George, but was soon at sea again en route for Palestine just in time for the British withdrawal, from what had now become something of a hot

186

spot with the beginnings of what we know today as terrorism.

Back in the UK at Colchester, work took a slightly alcoholic turn with employment in the Officers' Mess, where he not only mixed a memorable punch for the Queen's visit but also armed with toothbrush and Eucryl toothpaste (who remembers it?) cleaned all the blackened regimental silver recaptured from the Japanese. During this time he also changed his paybook status from single to married.

In mid July 1949, some sabre rattling around Hong Kong by the Chinese caused a little unrest and a general extension of service and from the bar at Colchester the view changed to that from an observation post on the Chinese border where things fortunately did not escalate.

However, not so in Korea where the Argylls as part of the UN force were called upon to 'help keep the peace'. Once again Arthur packed his kit and for the next seven months he experienced all and even more that life facing such an enemy could bring and is related in his story.

Return to Hong Kong followed for another spell and then finally home again where after seven years and one hundred and five days his service to the Crown terminated.

Civilian life began where it had left off at Coventry where for the next thirty two years with the Rover Group he helped produce such memorable names as the Hillman Minx, Hunter and Humber Snipe. Eventually with the decline of the motor industry those became casualties and Arthur became self employed as a fabricator of aluminium doors and windows. Life again changed dramatically in 1999 with the sad loss of his wife and seven years later in 2006 he proudly put his cap badge up again, but this time on the cap of the Royal Hospital.

Put a Sock in it
Arthur Masters

Korea has been described as a strange mixture of a country resembling Kashmir, Baluchistan with the Arakan thrown in for good measure and an equal mix of climatic conditions. Needless to say we arrived in 1950 ill equipped for any of them and found ourselves facing the 'Gooks' who boasted quilted jackets, warm headgear and boots built for the terrain whilst we still sported jungle green and our vehicles and carriers had seen better days. Things only improved when the later drafts arrived with new equipment, but it was thanks to the Yanks that we enjoyed the benefits of better kit, the famous K rations and of course the omnipresent PX facility. Photographs taken at the time show us all wearing the distinctive and more serviceable woolly hat rather than the tin variety whilst our traditional 'Balmoral' would have fallen prey to souvenir hunters.

The nickname 'Gook' entered the Army vocabulary I think rather sadly from the transposition of the south Korean friendly greeting which we heard as 'me Gook' and assumed meant 'I am a Gook' which became associated with the Northern Koreans whose greetings were far from friendly.

This welcome I first encountered outside Pusan where we were out on the perimeter of the unit and so the first to be in contact with the enemy. I didn't actually see any of them but was more than aware of the hand grenades they welcomed us with. These deadly weapons shaped like circular cigarette tins were of Russian origin and contained slivers of metal that cut through anything. Indeed one of our chaps was seriously wounded in the back during an attack and lay for 24 hours before being recovered.

He survived bleeding to death by taking off his sock and stuffing it into the wound where the blood congealed and thus saved his life.

After this we moved our Vickers 5 guns forward. Here I must say that we gunners weren't always popular for the presence of our continuous fire would draw that of the enemy and make life rather difficult for the other blokes. Anyway we 'stood to' the next night when they paid a return visit and attempted a pincer movement – however, without success, but with heavy casualties and the award of the MM to our Sergeant for his part in the action.

Looking back it always seemed wet and cold and of course we could not light any fires for fear of giving our position away. It was this rain that nearly added to the casualty list for the wetness had seeped everywhere even into my rifle which on firing caused the barrel to bellow or balloon out with a more than painful kick back to my shoulder. The former was eventually repaired by the armourer but I had to heal myself!

On another occasion my prayers were answered in rather an unusual way. We were holed up in a ravine under heavy mortar fire and really expecting the worst, hence my prayers for survival – when a message came through informing me of all things that I had been promoted to L/Cpl – what a time to choose – and I did survive!

Prayers of another sort were offered up by my family at home when having no news of my whereabouts in the Army they opened the Coventry Evening Telegraph to see the headline 'Local Man in Korea' with my story splashed all over it. This in fact came from a press visit to the front and one of the journalists asking me about my home town and passing the story on – though not the best news at that time for a wife and mother to read.

As mentioned earlier the weather was a huge factor in our lives and I will never forget waking up one morning after a heavy fall of snow which had covered us as we slept to see everybody rising from their snowy beds and looking like a painting of the Resurrection by somebody like Stanley Spencer.

Gooks by name and Gooks by nature, they were very clever in infiltration, often disguised as peasants in white robes which concealed weapons. On one occasion whilst digging-in somebody called out that some Koreans were approaching and a huge man dressed in white appeared and was as our

Cpl thought not what he seemed to be. So drawing his pistol he fired at the man – totally missing him but at the same time deafening me with subsequent hearing loss which I have to this day.

However, life wasn't all Gooks and grenades. We did enjoy an enormous spirit of camaraderie not only amongst ourselves but also with the other nations involved including the free beer from the Canadians to the football against the Australians – but as for the 'peace-keeping', I leave it to you.

Roy Prisley
Royal Sussex Regiment

Born at Woolwich in 1931 Roy had what one could call an eventful childhood. After the departure of his father from the family, his mother as a single parent had the job of providing for him and his sister. This coupled with the exigencies of the times and the later bombing of London proved quite a problem. Eventually leaving school like so many at 14 he became a 'bobbin boy' in the ropery of the Royal Naval Dockyard at Chatham for which he received the sum of £1.20 for a 48 hour week.

Later an encounter with gypsies brought about a dramatic change in his life as you will read and it was from their world that he enlisted in the Royal Sussex Regiment and began his 20 years and 11 months service with the Colours.

After basic training and now re-badged into the Middlesex Regiment he found himself off to Korea to 'keep the peace'. A taste of the battlefield, a shrapnel wound and a L/Cpls stripe thrown in for good measure were the results.

A tour of Egypt followed back with the Royal Sussex, and riding shotgun on the railways carrying oil between Egypt and Kenya, with shades of T.E. Lawrence. In 1953 the regiment returned to the UK to march in the Coronation procession. March it certainly was, for with a petrol strike in progress the only way to reach London was by foot so the regiment with band playing marched from Bulford in Hampshire over five days to play their part. Playing a part of a different and less glamorous sort then followed in Kenya during the Mau Mau problems, and thence back to Minden in Germany for demob in 1954. But not for long, for in 1958 he put on his uniform again with the Royal Sussex and once more began globe trotting Gibraltar and Libya returning to Bulford in 1959. However, it was back to the sunny skies above Malta in 1963 during which time the emergency in Aden found the regiment called there on duty.

1968-70 was spent with BAOR at Lemgo during which time after discussion he switched his career path to one in the officers' mess little knowing the eventual outcome. Thus at Aldershot under the tutelage of a former Royal Major Domo he mastered the intricacies of the etiquette of table laying, menus, wine selection and costs and staff control. Even in the field he took two marquees, 40ft. of carpet, tables, silver, crockery, napkins and waiters in mess kit – who says style is dead? After five years in this role he then went on a course as General's House Sergeant and as such worked for General Dean Drummond and General Blacker. In 1974 fate took another dramatic turn and he was appointed Major Domo in the household of the Queen Mother at Clarence House about which his lips are sealed, finally being demobilised in 1977.

After all this, civvy life did not suit him. Thoughts of a career as a butler did not materialise and he became a school care-taker but for only six months. His application to be Chief Steward at the RE Officers Mess Strood was accepted, but after six months the job was centralised at the Royal School of Military Engineering at Chatham and the post was made redundant, but with the same grade he was given the post of Senior Storekeeper in the Plumbing Section and as such remained for 25 years until retirement at 65.

The military world still played a part in his life especially military history and his involvement in a group portraying the 42nd Black Watch – and the joining of which produced momentary panic in his wife who thought he had joined up again. With them for 6 years he played a part in re-enactments at Waterloo, Corunna etc. Following the death of his wife Betty in 2001, it was the call of the Army again and in March 2002 after applying to Chelsea he proudly marched through the gates, but as you will read without a gypsy escort this time!

Gypsy Boy to Major Domo or Caravan to Clarence House
Roy Prisley

When I think of my early childhood I realise not only would it be impossible to live like that to-day with all the regulations but it also at times seems to be a mixture of Dickens and Ripping Yarns!

Home life was difficult and unhappy and after leaving school at 14 I found work as a 'bobbin boy' in the Ropery of the Chatham Dockyard. My sister Joy and I kept rabbits and used to go out to collect grass for them and on one occasion encountered two gypsy boys about our own age. After a rather physical and violent introduction with fists flying we became great friends and they not only introduced us into the gypsy way of life but in those days of wartime food shortage showed us how we could live off the land by catching pheasants, rabbits finding mushroom and even catching lobsters and crayfish etc. on the Isle of Grain. We even tasted the gastronomic delight of 'fizzy pig' in other words hedgehog cooked in clay which tasted just like rabbit.

Our relationship grew and with the bonus of fresh food my mother finally approved of our friendship so when we asked if we could go with our friends for three months hop and fruit picking in Kent she agreed – partly due also to the fact that she was now courting. What an experience – hard work but rewarding. We slept in hoppers' huts on straw pallets and at night had sing songs round the fire. After the hops we moved on to strawberries, apples and pears. These we picked by climbing into the trees whilst the men stood below, – no health and safety then. At the end I returned home with £300 in my pocket and news that my mother was to marry. Her future husband not only an unpleasant man but one who had been physically violent to me – so with her consent once more I left home and joined my gypsy friends – this time permanently.

And these years were the happiest of my life, just think of it no school, plenty of food and carefree life, travelling the country, visiting horse fairs and shows, the sort of existence that any young boy would envy. My eighteenth birthday arrived and with it the responsibility to do my National Service. One day a nosy policeman stopped me and asked for my papers etc. with the result that I was banged up overnight, given a medical which I passed and later received my call up papers and told to report to Chichester Barracks on December 2nd 1950.

My friends were horrified at the news and offered to help hide me and escape my duties, but I insisted on fulfilling my obligation and agreed to go and they said they would come and see me off.

See me off – indeed they did – the Guard at Chichester Barracks had probably never seen a new recruit arrive with four caravans and various children, dogs and all the other paraphernalia that travellers carry. The immediate reaction from the Guard Room was the threat of an attack. They turned out, rifles at the ready, main gates slammed and the Provost Sgt. advancing towards the caravan to find out what was happening. By then a crowd had gathered to watch the proceedings which became even more far-cical so much so that the Sergeant fuming with rage lost his temper, the crowd now of fifty or more roared with laughter at this and he in desperation threw his hat into the air only to see it land amongst the urine and manure that had been deposited by my caravan retinue. Things got even worse when his polished boots slipped on the mess and he like his hat ended up on the ground. Such was the chaos that followed and the arrival of the local press that the RSM appeared to take command not only of the situation but of me and I was finally marched off – not only to join the Royal Sussex Regiment but also to have a jolly good clean up leaving the Guard and the Sergeant to do likewise. So began my military career and the end of my gypsy life. Not quite, however, for how proud I was to see them all turn up for my passing out parade after basic training all spruced up and a real credit to me who was proud to introduce them to the RSM this time in different circumstances.

My next adventure, one of many during my service was perhaps the most traumatic for from being a new recruit I became almost immediately a fighting soldier in Korea where we were sent as part of the UN force. I had been trained as a Vickers Heavy Machine Gunner and the operative word was heavy – 40 lbs. for the tripod, 50lbs. for the water filled barrel, plus ammo and our own kit which was split between two of us. After two days marching to where the regiment was dug in the mountains, I was told to take over as No. 2 gun to relieve a Cpl who had been standing in for the previous gunner who had been killed – not an auspicious start.

Our kit was unsuitable for the country, jungle green battle dress etc. whereas the Chinese had quilted jackets, good boots etc. and thank goodness for the Americans who in fact shared their equipment with us.

In the next two years I faced all that the North Koreans could throw at us. We hiked from mountain to mountain or laagered down rock reinforced trenches fighting them off. Sometimes rather like today's film epics they would appear in the thousands blowing bugles and whistles, and although our gun took out very many at times it actually came down to hand to hand fighting. One of the saddest events took place on March 29th 1950 when Pte John Sharp my No. 2 got killed. We were sheltering from heavy shellfire when one landed 5 feet in front of our laager; the blast picked us up and blew me across the laager. I landed not too lightly amongst the rocks narrowly missing our gun that had also been hurled into the air but was undamaged. I said to John 'They are getting a bit near, I wonder what's got their goat' but received no reply. On crawling over to see him I found him dead with a piece of rock buried in his head. Although we had only known each other for a short time we had almost become like brothers – brothers in arms you could say, and only a matter of feet had separated me from the same fate.

We buried him where he fell with a small wooden cross, but not alone for nine others lost their lives that day. Later his remains were transferred to the UN memorial Cemetery at Pusan, South Korea, but 22654980 Pte J. Sharp South Staffs will be remembered not only by me but also now by those of you who read this story.

Wally Offord
The Royal Signals

Wally Offord describes his life as 'full' and this is no exaggeration. His father had fought at the Battle of Omdurman in 1898, was a veteran of the Boer War, RSM of the 1st Battalion The Northumberland Fusiliers and a survivor of the battle of the Somme where only six officers and 25 other ranks out of a battalion of 700 survived the first day. Wally was born in 1917 at Littlehampton, Sussex, where his mother had moved while her husband was away at the war. He was educated locally and still remembers the day in 1927 when the school paraded in fours at Arundel Castle to celebrate the Duke of Norfolk's 21st birthday. This was in the days when they had half an hour of drill every day under the headmaster.

Wally always boxed, having started as a boy at 14, and remembers booth boxing on the Hog's Back and having to stand against old pros for three minutes for a flyer (perhaps £200 in today's money). He continued to box at light middleweight at unit level until the war intervened. The shape of his nose bears witness to his activities in the ring.

Wally left school at 14 and joined the Army as a Boy, becoming an Apprentice in 1932. Although in the Royal Signals, he was trained as a vehicle mechanic and remained so all his service. In 1936 he was posted to Egypt to the Command Signals headquarters in Cairo and remained there until the outbreak of war. During this time he was attached to the Survey Section and was engaged in making maps of the Western Desert, visiting the Oases of Kufra and Siwa, amongst others, much to the later benefit of the Long Range Desert Group and the SAS. Wally came to know a number of the characters in both organisations. As a vehicle mechanic his services were much in demand as they traversed the desert in their 15 cwt trucks as were his skills on the sun compass.

The outbreak of war saw Wally attached to the Royal Sussex at the boom defences at Suez and having been hospitalised for 3 months after a motorbike accident (he was a despatch rider at the time) he was posted to the Western Desert Signals Regiment in Alexandria. He took part in General Wavell's big push against the Italians and spent

Christmas 1940 in Benghazi from where his signals squadron were sent to Greece in early 1941, which the Germans had just invaded. There he was attached to the 2nd/8th Australian Infantry who were all but wiped out at Grevena Pass, before withdrawing to Athens through columns of refugees and being strafed from the air. He reckons he has done about the fastest marathon in history, driving his 15 cwt truck pursued by half the German army the 24 miles from Marathon to Athens in 35 minutes!

A move to Syria followed, to fight against the Vichy French as part of Paiforce, after which they moved to Bombay before he was sent home in June 1943, having served seven years overseas. Wally was clearly suffering from stress deprivation because before long he had volunteered for airborne training and completed his jumps at Ringway and Hardwick Hall. Early in the morning of June 6th 1944 saw him jumping over Normandy with a section tasked with setting out Eureka landing lights for the gliders on previously identified landing zones. They fought for a month before breaking out of the perimeter and returned to England in September. On Christmas Eve 1944 they were warned at short notice to be ready to move and shortly after found themselves supporting the Americans in the Ardennes in what became known as the Battle of the Bulge.

Wally's last operation was to jump at Wesel as part of the Rhine Crossing in March 1945, after which they advanced northwards ending up meeting the Russians at Mecklenberg. A posting to Palestine followed still with 6th Airborne Division Signals for over two years and in August 1948 Wally was sent to the 3rd Hussars at Lübeck, from whence he returned to 2 Div Signal Regiment at Hilden. In 1953 Wally transferred to REME, attended an Armament Artificers' Course at Arborfield and was promoted WO1. In June 1957 he was posted to BAOR at Bochum for two years and was finally discharged in April 1960 after 25 years with the colours.

Never one to relax, Wally joined the Iranian Oil Company as workshop supervisor at Ahwaz in 1960 where he stayed for four years, before becoming a transport fitter at London Airport for 12 years. In 1976 he became a school technician in Staines before retiring to Cambridgeshire in 1982. He nursed his invalid wife for 15 years and when she died in 1999 he found himself very much alone. It was not a difficult decision for Wally to make to join the Royal Hospital which he did in 2004.

No Time to Hang About!
Wally Offord

Having arrived in Egypt in 1936 and initially I had been posted as technician to a wireless station called Polygon outside Cairo. As my duties were not particularly onerous I found myself doing more and more work for the Survey Section because I was a vehicle mechanic by trade and knew how to drive. We were engaged in mapping the Egyptian (as opposed to the Libyan) Desert and in perfecting the sun compass. We generally set out in two civilian cars (Fords I think, with little thin tyres) and spent a week or two at a time in the desert. I would be directed to drive in a certain direction while the supervising Sergeant kept the two vertical pins of the sun compass in line and the shadow on the correct mark on the setting disk in order to follow the desired direction as the sun moved across the sky. It always felt as if we were moving in a gigantic arc. Our trips took us to Mersah Matruh on the Egyptian Libyan border and northwards to the coast and Fort Capuzzo. I remember meeting up with patrols of the 11th Hussars, the first troops in Egypt to be mechanised with their Rolls Royce armoured cars. The RAF had them too and used to patrol the thousand-odd miles to Baghdad. Major BB Kennett was my OC and had known me as a Boy. The sun compass needed a different brass setting plate for each day and we carried these around with us wherever we went. Gradually these were developed and made smaller and handier.

Once war had been declared we were able to range much further afield and came across Major Ralph Bagnold, the founder of the Long Range Desert Group and all his fellow officers – though of course they were far senior to us, mere private soldiers. We visited the oases at Siwa and Khufra, Jalo and Al Ageila, all of them hundreds of miles from our home base in Cairo and which of course were to come into their own as operating bases for the LRDG.

Greece was fast and furious. We arrived in early 1941 and were attached to the Australians. We advanced to Elasson (near Mt Olympus) where we remained for a couple of weeks until the Germans advanced and we were ordered to fall back. On one occasion we were to meet up with a party detailed to get the boy King Peter of Yugoslavia out of the country but the rendezvous never took place. It was at Larissa that we saw our first tank parked up by the side of the road having a brew. I remember thinking 'that's bloody funny, I didn't know we had tanks here,' and it was only when we drew level we saw the crew were all wearing jackboots! We floored the accelerator and were round the corner before they could react. Athens had been declared an open city to prevent damage and there was a cease fire. We had to get rid of all our sets, including a very expensive US-made Hallicrafter which we pushed off the roof of the hotel where it was positioned. It made a very satisfying mess when it hit the ground! We made our way to Argos Bay just in time to see our ship, the 'Ulster Prince' being bombed out of the water, but fortunately we were taken off by the Royal Navy at Kalamata.

Safely back in Egypt, it wasn't long before we were ordered to Syria, still with the Australians, and were engaged in chasing the Vichy French out of Beirut. They conducted a fighting withdrawal and things got quite warm for a bit, but eventually we took over their wireless station (named Radio Orient –

a French Army broadcast station) at Bamdoun. After a couple of weeks it was back to Palestine via Nazareth for a short spell and then off to Persia. We spent some months in mid 1942 building up communication links and visited Kirkuk and Mosul and in mid 1943 I was sent back to Blighty having completed seven years' overseas service.

They were looking for volunteers for the airborne and I thought, well, anything for a laugh! So I found myself on the night of 6th June 1944 hunched up in a Stirling bomber on my way to France. We jumped a few minutes after midnight and landed near Troan, three or four miles from our intended DZ at le Bas de Ranville. On our way back we assisted in the positioning of Eureka landing lamps for the incoming glider force which were being set out by the French, who had already lost a lot of men. We got to the RV in a quarry and met up with General 'Windy' Gale, the Commander of 6th Airborne Division. My Squadron Sergeant Major had smashed his pelvis on landing, so I filled in. There was fierce resistance when the gliders came in and they took a lot of casualties. We were stuck in Ranville for about a month before the breakout and I remember a couple of incidents. We had jumped with only a 24 hour ration pack and after a couple of days we were pretty peckish. An airdrop of rations was organised and down came these panniers, landing in full view of the enemy. I got a couple of lads and a jeep and we went off to collect this stuff. It was a laborious process hauling these panniers lying pretty much flat to avoid getting shot, but eventually we managed and arrived triumphantly back with the goods. You can imagine our disbelief on opening the first container to find it full of blasted chevrons! On another occasion a truck full of ammo had been hit and caught fire and I managed to jump into the cab, ram it into gear and steer it downhill towards the Caen Canal before jumping clear. Fortunately it worked and the fire was extinguished. On another occasion I recall an 'O' Group which included General Gale, Brigadier Lord Murray (1st Airlanding Brigade), Brigadier Lord Lovat (45 Commando) and Brigadier Hill (3rd Para Brigade). I was making a cup of tea nearby when Lord Lovat turned to his French ADC and said 'don't just stand there, man, give him (me) a hand, he's making you a cup of tea.' So this French officer kindly helped dig my slit trench!

On Christmas Eve 1944 we were having a bit of a party in barracks at Bulford when we were put on immediate notice to move. Within hours we were back in Europe crossing the River Meuse on our way towards Dinant. In the Ardennes we met lots of Yanks coming the other way and they all advised us not to go any further as there were Germans 'up there'. They didn't seem too demoralised, but it was a confused situation all the same. It had snowed a lot which prevented our aircraft from supporting us at low level. I was a despatch rider at this time. It was freezing cold and the roads were treacherous with ice. I remember when it thawed we saw the bodies of literally hundreds of dead Germans who had been completely buried under the snow. It was quite a sight.

Having been sent back to England with some vehicles I rejoined my unit by jumping at the Rhine Crossing and not long afterwards we linked up with the Russians. They were complete savages – most of them had never seen a flush toilet in their lives – and their treatment of the locals, women in particular, was nothing short of barbaric. We rescued a few women and I can recall seeing Russian soldiers drinking red petrol straight out of a motorbike petrol tank. When the war in Europe finished we were earmarked for the Far East but the dropping of the

Atomic Bombs stopped that and we finished up in Palestine trying to keep the peace between the Arabs and the Jews. There was a café in Haifa – Spinney's, I think it was – where we used to go and have a drink of a Friday afternoon and both sides would observe a cease-fire when we went down and on our return. Otherwise they were going at each other hammer and tongs! I was in Jerusalem for a time and went to the Wailing Wall as a tourist when I heard a voice behind me say ''ere, mate, got a Woodbine?' I turned round and saw this orthodox Jew with a black hat and ringlets and all. He had deserted in the Western Desert in '42 and had been on the run ever since. Poor little blighter, I don't smoke.

Frank Buttifant
The Royal Signals

Buttifant is an unusual name, possibly stemming originally from the French 'Buttevant' which appears first in the 12th Century. Whatever the origins, a Sir John Buttevant was appointed Treasurer to the King's Purse in 1678. Gordon Brown, watch out!

Frank was born in Norwich in 1916, the youngest of three children. His father had served as a farrier, possibly (thinks Frank) in the Royal Norfolks, in the First War and came home a broken man. Frank did well at local school in Norwich and was set to go on to better things, but his mother (who had shouldered the burden of earning for the whole family), could not afford the French, Greek, Latin and Maths books, so he left school at 14 and after various jobs joined the local branch of Debenham's stores in the advertising department, mostly designing posters – he had enrolled some time before at the City of Norwich Evening Art School.

During the 30s Frank joined the local TA

regiment, the 4th Norfolks, and having learned a good deal of signalling (Morse at 18 words per minute, flags and wireless, and with one stripe) it was clear that on call up in 1939 that he was destined for the Royal Signals. He duly trained in a number of skills and was posted to the Lanarkshire Yeomanry, an artillery regiment equipped with 4.5 inch howitzers, as part of the signals detachment. He recalls that all the officers rode and that the Colonel wore a monocle.

In the autumn of 1941 they sailed east in a 30-ship convoy with Royal Naval escort via Capetown and his was one of the five ships directed to Bombay, from whence they were transferred to the Indian Army in the shape of the 11th Indian Division. They landed at Port Swettenham in northern Malaya and Frank's job as part of the signals troop was relaying instructions from the OP to the gun line. At this time (September 1941) there was no enemy, though the Japanese were certainly making belligerent noises. The regiment (155 Field Regiment RA) moved north to Sungei Patani just south of the Siam border where they heard the news of the Japanese attack on Pearl Harbor on 7th December 1941. A 70-day fighting withdrawal the 500 miles to Singapore down the western side of Malaysia, followed the Japanese landings on the eastern side of the country and their subsequent thrusts southwards. Frank's unit was engaged in no fewer than 6 set-piece battles during this time. The Japanese could take any amount of punishment from machine guns and small arms, but they hated the artillery, and this fact was to play a significant part in Frank's wartime experiences.

They arrived in Singapore in time to witness the burning oil depot by the docks and on the 15th February 1942 the garrison surrendered. His small section of signallers had found themselves shelter in an (empty!) brothel, but decided to try and find a boat to escape, having destroyed all their signals equipment and buried the bolts of their rifles. They found one and were about to embark when they were challenged by a British sentry who would undoubtedly have opened fire if they had proceeded any further. Bizarrely, there were 1000 British soldiers who, under the terms of the sur-render, were still employed to keep order before the Japanese entered Singapore, a fact that does not appear in any official accounts.

Finally they were gathered together and marched the 18 miles to Changi Prison where they were crammed 10 men into two-man cells. Fortunately this did not last long. At length in November 1942 they were put on board a ship and taken to Formosa (present day Taiwan) when for two and a half years Frank worked in the infamous Kinkaseki 'slave' copper mine. Copper was a colour that heavily influenced his time under the Japanese for Frank was ginger-haired and his captors always felt that 'the ginger haired one' was cooking up some nefarious plan and often singled him out for special treatment.

In 1945 Frank and his fellow prisoners were liberated by the Americans and eventually arrived back home in a hospital ship in late 1945. To add insult to injury the wife he had left behind had taken up with an American soldier and had had his baby. Frank did, however, find his soul mate in the shape of Audrie, a RHN sister who looked after mentally unbalanced patients, and they were married not long afterwards. Frank himself became a psychiatric nurse at the Hellesdon Hospital just outside Norwich and remained there until his retirement in 1981. Sadly, Audrie had died not long before and after trying Malta as a suitable retirement location, he returned home three years later. In spite of the comforting attention of his wife's children, Franks retirement was lonely and beset with illnesses and medical problems directly attributable to his treatment at the hands of the Japanese and he decided to come to the Royal Hospital where he has been since January 2003.

Chichi Roko – Number Seventy Six
Frank Buttifant

After Singapore had surrendered the Japanese had no idea how to deal with the enormous number of POWs. We spent several months at Changi Prison and at River Valley Camp in Malaya where one of the things we had to do was to construct a Jap war memorial at Bukit Tima. It was during this time we started to get an inkling of what the future might hold for us as prisoners of the Japanese. Food was short, the work was hard and we were clouted freely.

Their plan for us was to set us to work and we were given various tests to ensure we were in reasonable physical condition (including a glass rod up the rectum). We embarked for Formosa in the hold of a steamer, several hundreds of us with little food, short of water and in steaming heat, arriving in Keelung, on

217

Friday 13th November. We were marched immediately the 15 miles to the camp at Kinkaseki, a terrible uphill journey and on arrival our boots were removed and labelled (I got mine back in 1945!) We were allocated a 'bedspace' 14 inches wide in long wooden buildings and issued two blankets. There was no other furniture. You could smell the copper sulphate in the humid air and the whole place had a forbidding feel. We were split into working parties under a 'honcho' (one of our own), and every night and morning we had to stand at attention by our bedspace and call out our number in Japanese – the Japs were for ever checking that we were all there.

Work started at 6 am or thereabouts with a parade often in the pouring rain and we set off armed with a small carbide lamp and a cigar-sized box of rice for the day. The rice usually went sour and uneatable by midday. We usually received a beating at the start of the day for failing to meet the previous day's work quota. Initially we had a long walk up and over the mountain to the mine entrance but after a year or so the Chinese engineers blasted a tunnel through the mountain which made it easier. We later discovered that in the event of an invasion we were to be marched into the tunnel and both ends sealed to disguise what had been going on – a mass grave.

On Formosa there were a total of 15 camps but it was only at Kinkaseki that the conditions were so harsh. We were gunners and the Japs hated us and made sure we paid for that. As injury and death took their toll at Kinkaseki replacements were sent in from the other camps. The Kinkaseki mine was a famous and valuable mine producing copper, gold and silver, the copper being shipped back to Japan for use in the munitions industry. Regular shipments continued until the Americans' intervention at sea made this impossible.

Conditions in the mine were terrible. It was constantly wet through the seepage of sulphurated water through the rock and there was a long maze of tunnels to be negotiated. We had to bow to a statue of some sort at the entrance and typically it took 30-60 minutes to get to the face. Once there we would be allocated alleyways to work in. During the night the Chinese engineers would blast the rock and it was our job to clear the fallen rock into trolleys, always fearful that a further rock fall would bury us – there were no props or supports and we could see it crumbling and shaking above our heads. We could only work in the worst 'holes' as we called them, for five or six minutes before fainting through heat and lack of oxygen. The heat in the deepest 'holes' ranged from 130 degrees to 150 degrees Fahrenheit and of course there was no ventilation at all. Our mates would pull us out and take our place for a similar time while we 'recovered' and pulled them out in turn. We worked in this fashion for twelve hours a day. Often during working a blast from somewhere else in the mine would blow out our lamps and we had to wait in total darkness for our Japanese overseer to come and relight our lamps. We had no matches ourselves.

These foremen were absolute so and so's – cruel, vicious and sadistic – and we grew to hate and fear them. They would beat us unhesitatingly and for no reason whatever with rifle butts or the wooden handles of the mining hammers used for loosening rock. They did everything they could to make our lives a misery. They themselves hated the mine and they took it out on the only people who couldn't retaliate – us. We had names for them – The Eagle, Goldie, The Ghost, Frying Pan, Pan Face and Blackie among others. Our clothes consisted of a loin cloth and simple plimsolls to protect our feet from the sharp rocks and stones. This did not prevent the sulphurous water from literally burning our feet. We were usually working in six inches of hot, stinging water which gradually turned the skin yellow. My feet still burn at night after more than sixty years. Every day was hell and every night full of dread as to what the next day would bring. You thought every day could be your last. Most nights, at the end of each day's work, we would be lined up, told to hold onto an overhead blasting pipe and repeatedly beaten for not producing sufficient ore.

One day a large rock crushed my foot and I was able to spend three blessed months out of the mine. Occasionally one of the guards would give my foot a playful bash with his rifle butt, but I didn't mind as it only prolonged my stay above ground. Incidentally, our footwear in camp consisted of a foot-long piece of wood with a leather cross strap cut from the uppers of a boot from a dead man.

Our doctors were simply fantastic. If it had not been for their unstinting efforts many more of us would have died or gone mad. Major Ben Wheeler, a Canadian, and Captain Peter Seed, RAMC did their best for us. Every evening the sick and injured paraded in front of them and they developed a system once they had examined us of giving us either a white card (fit for work) or a red one (unfit, providing our 'hosts' agreed). Apart from mining injuries our main complaints were from wet beri-beri when your whole body swelled up like the Michelin man and you could hardly walk, and dry beri-beri when you evacuated all the liquid and your body shrank to matchstick thinness. The smell of death was everywhere.

From time to time we used to get faint whisperings of goings-on in the outside world through our very rare contacts with the local Chinese, villagers or engineers, most of whom seemed kindly disposed to us – they used to call us 'long noses', and it was through this that we finally heard the war and our long agony was over.

We were finally rescued by the Yanks who looked huge to our eyes and I recall they could hardly believe their eyes at the state of us. One of them actually fainted at the sight of us!

I am often asked whether I hate the Japanese and the answer is that I cannot hate the modern generation who had nothing to do with our circumstances. But their grandfathers? That's a different matter.

The publishers hope that this book has given you enjoyable reading. Large Print Books are especially designed to be as easy to see and hold as possible. If you wish a complete list of our books please ask at your local library or write directly to:

Dales Large Print Books
Magna House, Long Preston,
Skipton, North Yorkshire.
BD23 4ND

This Large Print Book, for people
who cannot read normal print,
is published under the auspices of

THE ULVERSCROFT FOUNDATION

... we hope you have enjoyed this book.
Please think for a moment about those
who have worse eyesight than you ...
and are unable to even read or enjoy
Large Print without great difficulty.

You can help them by sending a
donation, large or small, to:

**The Ulverscroft Foundation,
1, The Green, Bradgate Road,
Anstey, Leicestershire, LE7 7FU,
England.**
or request a copy of our brochure for
more details.

The Foundation will use all donations
to assist those people who are visually
impaired and need special attention
with medical research, diagnosis
and treatment.

Thank you very much for your help.